# Heartbroken
## YET BARKSTRONG

### A JOURNEY THROUGH SIBLING GRIEF

Kim Bark White

Copyright © 2024 by Kim Bark White.

All rights reserved. No part of this publication may be reproduced, distributed, or transmitted in any form or by any means, including photocopying, recording, or other electronic or mechanical methods, without the prior written permission of the publisher, except in the case of brief quotations embodied in critical reviews and certain other noncommercial uses permitted by copyright law. For permission requests, contact the publisher at the website address below.

Author: Kim Bark White.

Website: mindful-empowerment.net

*Heartbroken Yet BarkStrong* / Kim Bark White. First edition.

The information contained in this book is for general information and entertainment purposes only. The recommendations, opinions, experiences, observations, or other information contained herein is provided "as is," and neither the author nor publisher make any representations or warranties of any kind, express or implied, about the accuracy, suitability, reliability, or completeness of this book's content. Any reliance a reader places on such information is therefore strictly at their own risk. All recommendations are made without guarantee on the part of the author and publisher. To the maximum extent permitted by law, the author and publisher disclaim all liability from this publication's use. In no event will either the authors or publisher be liable to any reader for any loss or damage whatsoever arising from the use of the information contained in this book. This book is not a substitute for professional services, and readers are advised to seek professional aid in the event of an emergency.

ISBN: 978-1-954479-03-6

# PRAISES

Kim's poignant narrative in *Heartbroken Yet BarkStrong* beautifully captures the raw emotions of grief and the journey towards healing after the loss of a sibling. With her heartfelt words, Kim artfully navigates through the pain, offering solace and understanding to those who may be experiencing similar struggles.

The book delves deep into the intricate layers of grief, portraying the rollercoaster of emotions that accompanies loss. Through Kim's candid storytelling, readers are invited to embark on a journey of self-reflection and resilience, ultimately finding strength in the midst of heartache.

*Heartbroken Yet BarkStrong* serves as a beacon of hope for anyone grappling with loss, offering comfort, guidance, and a sense of solidarity in the healing process. Kim's words resonate deeply, reminding us that even in our darkest moments, we have the power to emerge stronger and more resilient than ever before.

If you're navigating the turbulent waters of grief, this heartfelt book is a must-read. Kim's profound insights and unwavering honesty will undoubtedly leave a lasting impact, offering a glimmer of light in the midst of darkness.

—Robin Fitzsimons

When presented the opportunity to read *Heartbroken Yet BarkStrong: A Journey Through Sibling Grief*, by Kim Bark White, I approached the book with equal parts trepidation and longing. I longed for a kindred soul, someone who would understand my grief. I dreaded the emotion I knew would come. My sister had passed just over twelve months prior to finding this book. I'd already navigated her birthday, the holidays, and the first anniversary of her death. Did I really want to dredge up those feelings again? What I found was the understanding I craved. White's elucidation of her feelings helped me define emotions that were still amorphous. I found comfort in the quotes scattered throughout the book, and left the work not feeling so alone. Kudos to the author for having the courage to pen her experience. I am grateful to have found this book. It is well written, and in my opinion, an asset to those who have lost a sibling.

—Tricia Copeland, Author of the Bestselling *Being Me* series

God is using Kim Bark White to reach those in the darkness that can accompany grief. This book is written in a way that facilitates a feeling of connectedness. The words on the pages are real, raw, and respectful. I strongly recommend this book as an invaluable resource. It has endless possibilities of helping people on many different levels of the grief spectrum. I personally will be using this book as a guide to help me improve the level of sensitivity in conversation when interacting with family and friends during different seasons of grief. Praise God for Kim Bark White and a wonderfully written book!

—Nancy Key

The book *Heartbroken Yet BarkStrong* explains the journey of one sibling finding her place after losing her brother. Watching Kim's "reality" first hand, I saw her complete devastation and how she fought to come back. Her grief guide is to help walk you through your sibling grief and lets you find *your* place in this grief process.

—Billiejo Hyer

Kim Bark White's book, *Heartbroken Yet BarkStrong: A Journey Through Sibling Grief* is a testament to how grief can weave its way into one's world without taking into account the havoc it will cause, the wreckage it will leave, and the emptiness that loss creates.

Kim beautifully paints a picture of the waves that come and recede, while intertwining the immense love she shared with her big brother, Duane. Though her story is a beautiful memorial to her "Big Bro" and the relationship they shared, I was able to relate to the intricacies of grief. *Heartbroken Yet BarkStrong* takes you on a journey of grief; how it can take you down and swallow you whole.

Grief has a way of giving you glimpses of hope that you may be able to survive this nightmare if only you hold onto your loved one's memory tighter and dream at night a little longer. And as the next morning arrives, you awaken with tear-filled eyes, a heart broken, and a memory you insist on keeping alive.

Kim gives us permission to sit in the grief, knowing there is no end but rather an invitation to dance with it. Thank you, Kim, for taking me on the journey of your own healing so that I too could heal a little more from the grief I have endured. Love truly never dies; therefore our loved ones are always by our side.

—Erin Baer, Best-selling Author | Speaker

I had goosebumps while reading this book. The author, Kim Bark White, displays so much raw, real emotion and vulnerability, it's impossible not to be affected. It's a truly incredible person who can take personal loss and tragedy and turn it into a way to help others. That is exactly what Kim Bark White has done with her book, *Heartbroken Yet BarkStrong*. Kim experienced the loss of her brother and searched for resources to help her through the grieving process of losing a sibling. Despite all of the books and resources on grieving, none seemed to fit the sibling grief Kim was experiencing. Seeing that there was a need for support specifically for sibling grief, Kim's book idea was born. She lays out all of the emotions she experienced, with nothing held back. Kim provides validation for the myriad of emotions grievers may experience and ways that she worked through her grief. The author explains that grieving is not a linear process, and everyone's grieving path will be different, and that's totally ok. Not only is this a book about grieving, more importantly, it is a book about hope and finding ways to honor the legacy of those we have lost. I cannot recommend this book highly enough! I know it will provide needed support and guidance for those who are struggling with the loss of a sibling. If you know anyone who is grieving a sibling, do them a favor and buy them this book!

—Amy Jones

Well written! Thank you for putting into words the good, the bad, and the ugly truths and surreal feelings that surface when dealing with such a loss.

—Peggy Beach

Wow, this book brings endless emotions to the surface! All while allowing the reader to sort through the emotions one goes through when losing loved ones. Kim has done such a wonderful job putting her raw emotions on paper while sharing the hardest days of her life with the utmost vulnerability to allow others to heal through their own grief.

I especially found the "reflections" exercises to be therapeutic, non-invasive, and completely relevant, while experiencing Kim's gifted writing.

—Sally Rech, Rech Family Gardens

Kim shares the very raw and real emotions and realities to be faced when dealing with the loss of a loved one. Kim's story has fully shown that there is no timeline or set schedule for healing from a loss. Life does not return to normal as it once was, and although life must go on, we learn to navigate life to a "new normal" way of living, never dismissing or forgetting what once was. Kim not only shares her journey but allows others to know that they are not alone as they navigate their own. When the time is right for you, take that step to begin your journey to healing.

Kim shares a very beautifully written story of how she has taken her grief and loss, and is driven to help others. In true Kim fashion, she continues to move mountains for all those she loves. I think her brother Duane continues to lead and watch over his sister. He most definitely said it best, "I've got your back Sis!"

—Missy Cornwell-Nichols, Wife, Mother, Nana, and Friend

I dedicate this book to my Big Bro, Duane who provided my heart and soul with the essence of us.

I dedicate this book to my fellow grievers who are faced with the reality of a sibling's death *and* to all those who are mourning the loss of someone you loved as well. May you find peace in your heart, hope for better days ahead, and a sense of joy again in your life.

## ABOUT THE COVER

I am so proud of this book cover. The photo depicts the essence of who Duane and I were as siblings; it's as if you can feel the love and soul connection between us. The background is a picture I took overlooking the farmland at our parent's house. This land was recognized as a Century Farm, and has now been in the Bark family for well over 100 years. This homestead and its Bark generations, have witnessed hardships and prosperity, sorrows and joy, despair and hope, and everything in between. Just like my ancestors, I too, have experienced the same. This is my heritage; it is where BarkStrong got its roots.

# INTRODUCTION

**WELCOME INTO MY GRIEF JOURNEY** world as I know it, from a sibling's perspective. It's here that I can sit with you, hold space for you and your emotions, gently let you know that I care, and ultimately take your hand and walk this journey along beside you. I've created this safe haven for you to cry, smile, find peace, have hope, and to let you know it's OK to feel what you're feeling. No judgment; just sincere compassion.

    I was born into a nuclear family of four, consisting of Dad, Mom, older brother Duane, and myself—the Barks. I *knew* how to live life *with* them in it; I *didn't* know how to do so without them in it. All my life, I've been my brother's sister; it's part of my identity, part of who I am. My brother is part of my past; we shared a common history. My life abruptly changed when my Big Bro passed away in 2020. I am intensely passionate about providing this resource for you, the sibling. I didn't know where to turn in the midst of my shattered world, and I promised myself that I'd turn my pain into purpose by bringing encouragement and light to my fellow sibling grievers. Your grief is real. Your grief is valid. I know, and I understand.

As a sibling griever, I felt my identity was less apparent to the outside world—mine was "disenfranchised" grief. I wasn't the spouse, wasn't the parent, and wasn't the child of the deceased. There is no word in the dictionary that labels the loss of a sibling.

> "If you lose a spouse, you're a widow or widower. If you lose your parents, you're an orphan. But if you lose a sibling, you just become the girl who lost her brother" (author unknown).

With no word or label, what was I? I had my own identity and wasn't sure where I fit in as a griever. Although each of these relationships have similar processes to work through on the grief journey, each griever title is also quite unique according to the role and/or title the deceased played in your life. I had to remind myself that even though there is no term for sibling grief, all grief is important. All grief has validity. And all the by-products of grief are hugely impactful to *all* those involved. My grief wasn't less than or more than anyone else's; it was "simply" *my* grief. And yours is too.

> "Grief—There is no hierarchy. One person's grief is not comparable to another's in any way that could make one loss greater or harder or make any other person's loss less valid" (excerpt from *Grief Rules/It's a Good Thing*).

I'm on a grief journey; there will never be a magical destination that says I've arrived and now it's over. Instead, I've learned to offer myself grace, knowing that grief is not linear but is an ebb and flow. Grief will now always be a part of my life because with the loss of my brother, my life has been forever changed.

# INTRODUCTION

> "There comes a point in life when you realize that nothing will ever be the same, and you realize that from now on, time will be divided in two parts—before this and after this" (www.livelifehappy.com).

I know that it won't hurt less; I just hope that it will hurt less often. Duane will always be imprinted in my soul. He will always be with me, like a handprint on my heart.

My life was a shattered mess, and I lived in that state of being for quite a while. I hit a fork in the road and had to make a decision—Would I spend the rest of my life in the pit of grief, wallowing around, or would I find ways to rise out of that pit with a purpose and a passion? Thankfully, I chose to take the narrow path of rising up; and I'm offering the same to you.

Unfortunately, there is no how-to manual when dealing with grief. But what I *can* offer you is a candid look into *my* life as a grieving sibling. I can share my thoughts, my worries, my stress, and my sense of hopelessness. But just as importantly, I can authentically share with you my ways of finding hope, joy, and peace in the midst of the greatest loss and sadness I've ever experienced. As you continue to read this book, my hope is that you find multiple snippets of my experiences that resonate with you. My pain does, in fact, have purpose when I am able to pour comfort into others who have been—or will at some point be—traveling a grief journey similar to mine. It is a lovely feeling to be able to share hope and peace with others who are hurting in the same way I have hurt.

> "The messy part of your story is probably the part that God will use the most to reach others" (author unknown).

Take a deep breath; allow yourself to feel whatever it is that's necessary. I'm not promising you easy, but I do promise to be right here beside you the whole way. I'll be your safe haven and your soft place to land when it feels like nobody else understands. Are you ready? Let's turn the page together.

# THIS IS US

"To my brother, you're the best friend I was born to have" (author unknown).

**WHETHER YOU ARE AN ONLY CHILD** or someone *with* siblings, I'm guessing you have that special someone who is your ride-or-die bestie. That person is either your real sibling or someone you're *so* connected with that they *feel* like your sibling. It's that person whom you wouldn't know how to do life without. It's that someone who knows everything about you, loves you unconditionally, has your back, encourages you, and protects you no matter what. It's with great pride and honor that I introduce you to my special someone, my Big Brother, Duane!—aka, Big Bro.

The Barks—two guys, two gals. Dad was a kind, gentle soul, with a quiet demeanor and a sly sense of humor. He spent his life teaching and coaching, having a positive impact on many lives during his fifty-plus years in those roles. He taught me biology in the classroom, but more importantly, he taught me how to be a compassionate and respectful human being in whatever arena I was in. When things got tough, or when we had to dig deep within during difficult situations, I remember Dad saying, "Give it the 'Bark Method.'" That was his way of letting us know that he believed in us, that we could do anything we set our mind to, and that he'd be right there supporting us along the way. He led by example and often let his actions speak louder than words. So when *I* heard, "I love you," I knew the depth of those three spoken words.

Mom is the social butterfly. She should own stock in Hallmark greeting cards because she is phenomenal at sending handwritten notes. It's a light day if she only has five envelopes in her mailbox waiting to be mailed. Whether it's birthday wishes, anniversary wishes, get-well wishes, or just brighten-your-day wishes, Mom's correspondence comes straight from the heart. Mom is a gold-medal contender in being a people person. Duane and I always joked that if she had dinner with a complete stranger, she'd have not only their whole life story but the life story of all their relatives by the time she left the table. Mom enjoys people, conversations, socializing, and giving to others in heartfelt ways.

> "The greatest gift our parents ever gave us
> was each other" (author unknown).

My brother Duane was my ride or die, my best friend, and my biggest fan. He spent his life doting on me and looking at me with pure adoration. We had a soul connection, and our mutual love and respect for each other ran deep. Duane had a heart of gold and would do anything for his family and friends. He took great pride in being a family man. He was a coach, school administrator, man of faith, and lived to make life better for others. Duane was all about making a difference for humankind. He led by example and earned the respect of many.

I like to think of myself as a combination of all three. As an empath, I'm kind, compassionate, and quite soft-spoken. I enjoy helping others become the best version of themselves. Faith is also important to me, and I have to say, it's God grace that got me to this place where I can reach out to help others on their grief journey.

> "She walked with God. That was her game-changing strategy" (author unknown).

Following in Dad and Duane's footsteps, I'm also an educator—teaching and making a difference for twenty-seven-plus years in a public school system. Although I've retired from that gig, I'm still teaching, but from a different platform, as I provide tutoring services to students and teach mindfulness classes to adults and children. Being the baby of the family, and a girl, I had myself wrapped snugly around my dad's and big brother's little fingers. I am the epitome of a "daddy's girl." As a toddler, I packed my blankie in his sleeping bag when Dad left for graduate school so that he wouldn't miss me. Our mutual love and respect ran deep as well.

> "Being a daddy's girl is like having permanent armor for the rest of your life" (Marinela Reka).

I'm also the doted on "Lil Sis." "Big brothers are the second-best blessings after father" (author unknown).

Dad and Duane were my rocks, my protectors, and my heroes. I was encouraged, guided, adored, doted on, loved unconditionally, and according to some, spoiled. How the heck was I supposed to figure out life without them in it?

Unconditional love was the common ground for our family's melting pot of personalities. "BarkStrong" was something we each personified and showed in our own unique ways. BarkStrong is a verb, it's something you do, it's how you act, it's how you love. Dad and Mom never sat us down to discuss BarkStrong; in fact, there wasn't even a term "BarkStrong" initially. We just grew up knowing its essence and how it felt to *live* BarkStrong. BarkStrong was this unspoken, unwritten concept that encompassed always having each other's back, always being there for each other, always supporting each other, always sticking up for each other, and always loving each other unconditionally. BarkStrong became a well-known term during Duane's Covid ordeal (more of his Covid story will come later). Our whole family of Barks drew closer and closer, leaning into the true meaning of BarkStrong as a family. In addition, we had prayer warriors and a whole BarkStrong network around the country, epitomizing what it meant to be BarkStrong. They had our back, supported us, and became our pillars of strength when it felt as though our foundation was crumbling. BarkStrong bracelets were the new accessories, BarkStrong yard signs were popping up everywhere, and #BarkStrong was a common sight.

"StayStrong. PrayStrong. BarkStrong" was how I ended my Facebook posts when updating everyone on Duane's latest highs and lows of Covid's wrath.

According to Mom, Duane and I had a special bond from the moment I came home from the hospital; this homecoming didn't occur for a month, however, because I was a preemie baby.

> "Between us is one thread: it ties our hearts, so we walk close to each other, always" (author unknown).

As I take trips down memory lane through photo albums, I can *feel* the love between us, and it melts my heart. There's the one photo where Duane is looking into the camera with a smile of pure pride and excitement while I sat in my pastel green-and-yellow infant seat gazing at him. Apparently, I innately knew from the beginning that he'd be my hero.

> "Some people don't believe in heroes. But they
> haven't met my brother" (author unknown).

Mom recalls the day when things seemed a little too quiet around the house. She was changing a load of laundry when Duane came bounding down the basement steps, full of pride, and blurting out, "Mommy, I shared with Kimmy!" Sharing a rattle or toy would have been a wonderful gesture for my less than two-month-old self. However, Duane decided to share some of his bubble gum with me! How sweet is that! I'm sure, on the inside, Mom's whole being immediately went into panic mode at that very moment, but knowing Mom and how she handles life, I have no doubt she gently and calmly (almost stoically) took care of the situation at hand. My Big Bro and I had an incredible, soul-level connection from the start, and I had no idea how to do life without him in it. If you have this book in your hands, you're probably also trying to navigate in a world that has been shattered because your sibling is no longer here with you.

How do I explain the feeling of nothingness, empty, dead inside, unenthused, and emotionless to others so they would understand? The best way I can explain it is through my writing. I've written this book in sections, as it makes more sense according to *my* healing process. The first section is a walk-through of the many stresses, worries, common "themes," negative emotions, and by-products I've encountered on my grief journey.

The middle section is my turning point from utter despair to deliberate and intentional hope. Then I'll share with you how I found glimpses of light inside the dark pit—light that is possible for you as well. Intertwined within these sections, I'll share my stories—real, raw, heartfelt, and authentically me. Then I'll give you some ideas of what not to do or say to those who are grieving and; instead, I'll offer some ideas that are more compassionate and helpful ways to support someone who is grieving. These are life lessons I've learned up close and personal as a griever. I truly believe that people offering their condolences do so with the best of intentions. However, after being on the receiving end, I've taken notice and have learned to handle my words and actions in a much different way as I reach out to those dealing with a loss of a loved one. In the last section, I'll give you an inside look at where I am now in my grief journey. Throughout this book, you will find many quotes (some with unknown authors and others with authors included). These quotes were there for me as if directly sent as a personal God tap for my heart at just the right moments. They resonated with how I felt in that instant. No one was experiencing my loss in the same way, and I wasn't able to adequately verbalize my feelings at the time; at least not in a way that others could fully understand my devastation. These powerful quotes somehow let me know that somebody, somewhere "understood," which brought me a hint of comfort and a smidge of strength to get through another moment.

Before we continue turning the pages together, let me say that I care, and my heart truly goes out to you. I know the enormous sense of sadness, the void, and the sheer hope of wanting life to be different than it currently is.

# IT WASN'T SUPPOSED TO BE LIKE THIS

"The irony of grief is that the person you most want to talk to about it is no longer here" (author unknown).

**WHEN THE RUG WAS PULLED OUT** from under me, there was a pile of shit to sort through, deal with, and wallow in emotionally, spiritually, and physically. I'm guessing you're currently sitting at the bottom of your grief pit sorting through the same kinds of rubble and wreckage; all while trying to do so without your go-to sibling.

"Brother: noun (bruth-er) a person who is always there for you when you need him; someone who picks you up when you fall; a person who stands up for you when no one else will; a brother is always a friend." (author unknown).

Duane and I did life together for our lifetime. Our love was immense, a connection deep within our souls. Crazy as it may seem, we didn't really fight;

instead, we always had each other's backs. "I got your back, Sis" was spoken a thousand times, a promise never broken. He was two years older than I, and as the years went by, I think he made it his mission in life to encourage, protect, guide, and love me through life.

> "When my brother didn't have my hand, he
> had my back" (author unknown).

He was my world, and I was his. He was my biggest fan, and I was his. Although we each had our own friends, we always came back to each other.

"A brother is better than one thousand friends" (author unknown).

It was in that safe haven that we had a mutual respect for each other and knew without a shadow of a doubt that our ride or die was each other. My Big Bro was the perfect combination of funny and serious. The smirk on his face when cracking a joke or poking fun at someone (usually, either at my expense, his wife Pam's, or Mom's) was sly and priceless. Duane would playfully poke fun at Mom, and I'd look across the way to see Dad with a tiny smile and a wink in his eye. Dad would want to laugh so badly but was never sure if it would be safe to do so because he didn't want to offend any of us.

Duane's annual Christmas letter brought the same kind of playfulness. Along with the typical catching up on the lives of their three children (Brad, Brian, Brittany) and their families, he'd expand on what was new with himself and Pam. However, not to have the letter be in total seriousness, he'd share humor, Duane Bark style. One year he told his readers he had opened a craft store in his garage, and anyone was welcome to come and shop. This was his way of teasing Pam for her love for decorating. It seems Duane thought they had plenty of decorative items and Pam certainly wouldn't miss a few things from her stash! On Pam's behalf, her knack for decorating is spectacular!

My Big Bro was also the epitome of calm, cool, and collected in times of serious matters. His life's career was in education. Those various roles, along with being the oldest child, needed his responsible, serious side. Whether he was informing his staff, taking care of discipline, heading up a board meeting, speaking to parents and community members, helping young athletes grow as people, or taking the lead with health concerns of our parents, Duane handled situations with the utmost respect, dignity, confidence, and fearlessness.

I assumed that he and I would grow old together, you know, until we were actually *old*. I'm guessing you were assuming the same in your life, too.

When Duane died in October 2020, my world literally shattered to pieces. (The roller coaster of his passing is a story for later.) The one person I needed to talk to most and be comforted by was no longer here.

> "My brother taught me everything, except how
> to live without him" (author unknown).

The following is the Facebook post I wrote the night he passed:

Oct 7, 2020, I am overtaken with a multitude of emotions tonight.

My heart is broken and I'm not sure how to navigate without my Big Bro; but I will figure it out because I Am BarkStrong!! I have the love and support of family and friends who will be by my side while I figure it out ~ gratitude.

There's a gut-wrenching sadness that rushes over me like ocean waves. I will figure out how to surf and ride the waves because that's what my Big Bro would want me to do.

I am empty. There is a void, a special place that will always belong to my Big Bro. But I know that that void will be protected and surrounded with the outpouring of love coming my way.

I am numb. It's as if I'm frozen in time and I can't go back yet I can't move forward. Perhaps the numbness is a blessing in disguise so that for now, the hurt doesn't hurt so bad. I've heard that the reason it hurts so much is because the love was so great. So much truth in that!

My heart is full of joy because I have a lifetime of memories etched in my heart and mind that I can pull from, like books on a shelf at any given moment. I am Blessed.

I am thankful that Duane is in Heaven with his Creator. I am confident my Big Bro was greeted with, "Well done, my Good and Faithful Servant." It doesn't get any better than that! I will be with him again someday; and we'll spend our eternity together. Duane is now pain-free and no longer struggling; and that brings me happiness, contentment, and peace of mind.

I am proud. What an impact Duane has had on so many people. He's an inspiration and has definitely left a legacy. Just imagine the impact we can have if we Are Duane's Ripple Effect in the world!

I am feeling a deep sense of protection. I know I have a Guardian Angel who will always have my back! "I got your back, Sis" is whispering in my ears.

Love ya, Big Bro 🖤🖤 ~ Always have. Always will.

The following is what "shattered" looked and felt like from my Lil Sis viewpoint; perhaps some of this is what you're experiencing too.

"Grief: an earth-shattering moment that you live
with for the rest of your life" (Mark Lemon).

# DOES SOMEONE HAVE A HOW-TO MANUAL, PLEASE?

"When a sibling dies, it is like a deep hole implodes inside of you. It's as if the hole penetrates you and leaves you gasping for air" (Alan D. Wolfelt).

Grief: noun (gref): a deep and poignant distress caused by or as if by bereavement, the state or fact of being bereaved or deprived of something or someone ... Grief is messy, hard, gut-wrenching, debilitating, and exhausting. Grief is not linear, not confined to a timeline, and it certainly does not follow a textbook's suggestions through specific stages ... Grief isn't tidy or predictable. Grief is as individual as love—every life, every path, is unique" (Megan Devine).

**GRIEF IS YOUR EXPERIENCE** and your experience alone. No two people experience grief in the same way or same time frame. There will never be a how-to manual for maneuvering through grief. There are, however, commonalities as we navigate this new norm. Your emotions, stresses, worries, reactions, responses, and feelings might not match mine exactly, but I'm guessing there are similarities. It might be the same types of emotions mirrored yet felt in ways that are deeply personal to you. These by-products of grief don't necessarily happen in order, and you can certainly be experiencing more than one at a time. Remember, it's OK to not be OK.

> "The only people who think there's a time limit for grief have never lost a piece of their heart" (author unknown).

My advice to you is to take the time *you* need during this most difficult time.

> "I asked grief, 'How long would she stay?' 'For as many days as you love them,' she answered. 'Then we will be sharing a lifetime together,' I said" (Deb Sheppard).

Again, there is no manual of instructions.

> "No rule book. No time frame. No judgment. Grief is as individual as a fingerprint. Do what is right for your soul" (author unknown).

In the following sections, I will walk you through the plethora of emotions I went through. At times, I felt these individually; at other times, I was overtaken by multiple emotions at once.

## Shock

Whether your sibling passed away suddenly or there was time leading up to it, there is a sense of shock that comes out of nowhere and smacks you across the face. For me, I had three grueling months to "prepare" myself for the possibility of no longer having my brother in my life. Who says that to a griever anyway? There is *no* such thing as "prepare" yourself, and if someone has the audacity to argue otherwise, you should probably throat punch them (or at least set them straight!).

The following is an excerpt from my chapter in the anthology *The Badass Within*

On October 6, Duane's wife, Pam called; as a family, they had decided to turn off the ventilator. There were no more options. He had suffered long enough. For three months, Duane fought the fight to no avail. As I heard those words, my heart shattered. They literally took my breath away. *How will I live life without him?"*

The next morning, I was still holding out hope. I was still praying that God had a miracle in store for our BarkStrong family, but that wasn't to be my reality. "Sitting in my living room, embraced by Mom and my husband, on October 7th by video call we watched Duane's last ventilated breath. My world was slowly crumbling. I didn't have my protector, my everything, to hold me in that moment." My heart and head were not in alignment; intellectually, I knew he was no longer here because I watched his last ventilated breath. Nonetheless, my heart wouldn't and couldn't come to terms with this truth.

> "Trauma is any sudden, terrible experience that disrupts your well-being and overwhelms you." (https://health.mit.edu/faqs/mental-health/common-reactions-to-traumatic-events)

> "A traumatic experience can shock your system, causing you to go into a state of dissociation, where your body and mind feel disconnected and nothing feels real" (Sanjana Gupta, "What Is Trauma Shock," 2022. verywellmind.com).

## *Reflections*

Are you in shock? Perhaps you feel dizzy, nauseous, and empty. Do you feel as though your mind and body have been disconnected? Are you walking around like a zombie, asking yourself, "Is this real?" For most of us, shock was an alarming jolt that blindsided us, and that was just the beginning of our tailspin.

## Numbness

Once my mind and body absorbed the shock, my next response was numbness. For me, the numbness was definitely linked to the dissociation. Maybe that's God's way of protecting us. The following is an excerpt from my Facebook post on the evening of Duane's passing.

> I am numb. It's as if I'm frozen in time and I can't go back yet I can't move forward. Perhaps the numbness is a blessing in disguise so that for now, the hurt doesn't hurt so bad. I've heard that the reason it hurts so much is because the love was so great. So much truth in that.

In the days following, I found myself just going through the motions, doing what needed to be done, operating on autopilot. I was experiencing emotional numbness but felt the need to put my grief on hold for a bit, to protect others. Be there for Mom. Be there for Pam. Be there for Brad. Be there for Brian. Be there for Brittany. Be there for their families. My main concern at the time was to make sure I was available (via phone or in person) and to do my best to ensure that they were OK. I felt it was my place to protect them; if the roles were reversed, my protector, Duane, would be doing the same for my family, with his typical 1,000 percent effort.

## DOES SOMEONE HAVE A HOW-TO MANUAL, PLEASE?

Let me take a moment to describe what *my* BarkStrong personal protector looked like. As the terms of endearment changed over the years from "Kimmy" to "Kim," "Lil Sis," or "Sis," the love and affection continued to grow stronger. Duane was the King Protector. In grade school, during recess, an older kid said something to Duane that was unkind, nasty, and unspirited about Mom. How dare that kid tell Duane his mom had big boobs! Duane had no option but to punch that mean bully—nobody messes with his Momma! Not even if the repercussions meant he'd have to go to the principal's office! Duane was ready and willing to suffer the consequences if it meant he would do what it takes to defend his mom! In high school, Duane had a chat with the principal, letting him know that his Sis *would* have a locker next to his. Upperclassmen had lockers in the center hub of the school and underclassmen had lockers on the perimeter of the school in the wings. As if that wasn't bad enough for Duane to deal with, the lockers were assigned alphabetically by last name; "Bark" was one of the farthest lockers away from the center hub where he was. Our principal, Dr. Butterfield, obviously couldn't produce a locker immediately, so Duane announced that he'd be sharing his locker with me until one opened up. It wasn't long, and guess what! I had a locker right beside my Big Bro's! Protection by proximity! Duane was also very protective of me when it came to dating. When he got wind on the football field, basketball court, in the locker room, or in the hallways that someone wanted to ask me out, his Big Bro mode kicked in. He screened my potential admirers, making sure *his* standards for *his* Lil Sis were met. Many dates didn't happen because Duane said, "Nope! She's not your date."

> "The best line a girl can say—You better watch out! I have a big brother, and I am not afraid to use him!" (unknown).

Now you can understand *why* I felt the intense need to protect Mom and Duane's family to the utmost of my ability; he fiercely protected those he loved, and I will forever do the same.

Once the shock and numbness dissipated, there were a multitude of other reactions, responses, negative emotions, and feelings that swarmed around me and consumed my being. Some days they came all at once, like being bombarded as the dodgeball target, and other days, I was swallowed up by only one or two.

"Grief is: Disbelief, Numb, frozen in time. Blank stares. Unable to think. Moving in slow motion, living in a fog. After the numb phase, when the thawing out begins, the pain settles in our broken hearts. In the meantime, the world expects us to function 'normally' in life" (Widows Hope Foundation).

## Reflections

The details of how these played out for me may not be exactly how it's been for you. However, the threads might sound familiar and resonate with your personal sibling grief story.

## Intense Sadness

"Sometimes it's very hard to release what's making you sad because it's the same thing that brought you so much joy" (author unknown).

There was an incredible and absurd sense of sadness that engulfed me. I had never felt this magnitude of sadness or sorrow before; it was like no other pain I'd ever experienced. I was consumed with sadness and tears. I remember wondering if my heart would always feel so intensely sad. The following is an excerpt from *The Badass Within*.

"Heartbroken": a compound word. You take the word heart and the word broken, and that's *exactly* it. That's what the intense sadness was; it was literally a broken heart. Sadness had absorbed itself into every cell of my body, like a sponge that was oversaturated. I cried; sometimes tears rolled uncontrollably down my face, and other times my body shook as if I was crying, but no tears flowed.

God hears tears as well as spoken words. I sank ever lower. I went through the motions, one foot in front of the other, but I was numb. Again. It felt paralyzing. I heard, "Keep the faith, Kim." I tried; I had so many talks with God, so many God taps were coming my way.

> "The tears in my eyes I can wipe away. The ache in my heart will always stay" (Healing Hugs).

## *Reflections*

Perhaps you've been experiencing intense sadness as well. Do you feel like there will *never* be a time that you'll feel joy or happiness again? Does it seem as if you'll be brokenhearted forever? Have you cried until there are no more tears; does that scare you? Are you questioning that if the tears stop, it means the memory is starting to fade? Are you worried you'll never be all right again?

## **Helpless**

Helplessness – Noun, marked by the inability to act, the feeling or state of being unable to help yourself or anyone else.

My sense of helplessness was not only at the time of Duane's passing and the grieving period after. It had previously been compounding daily during his three-month hospitalization with Covid. As you all know, everything shut down, and we were all isolated from our own families, unless they lived in our household. Covid stipulations, rules, and regulations kept me away, kept me secluded from Duane, and bore down heavily on my awareness of helplessness. The weight of all that powerlessness nibbled away at my being like a parasite feeding on me from the inside out. Please allow me to be vulnerable and rewind for a bit, as I reveal my gut-wrenching experience with my complete inability to help.

The following is an excerpt from *The Badass Within*.

July 2020, in the midst of the Covid-19 pandemic, three family members were Covid positive and hospitalized. Unfortunately, Duane ended up testing positive too. Wanting to spare our mom from worry, he said, "Don't tell her yet," hoping it would be a mild case. Each day, I noticed his breathing was becoming more labored during our chats. "Get to the doctor," I begged. He ignored my concerns. *If he was hospitalized, how could he take care of his loved ones?* Duane was admitted to the hospital, on his 61st birthday, and immediately taken to the intensive care unit (ICU). My world shook, but we continued to talk via phone and FaceTime. He was still protecting me, saying he'd be fine. Our conversations continued, reassuring each other of our love. He promised he'd be okay. I promised I'd have his back and help him fight. My heart was heavy, my gut felt nauseous. He was three hours away, and I felt helpless. I wanted to be in that ICU holding his hand and hugging him. I wanted to comfort him with a kiss on the forehead. Covid regulations dictated I couldn't be there. Being a woman of faith, I prayed, remaining hopeful he'd in fact be okay. Days became weeks, and things weren't improving. Our conversations continued but decreased in length. His energy was consumed with breathing. I was petrified and didn't know what to expect. I knew a fast decline could happen at any moment, leaving me dizzy and disoriented.

In early August, my brother and I had our last two-way conversation, minutes before he was placed on a ventilator and in an induced coma. I tried to be brave and not cry when he asked me for a favor. "Absolutely. What do you need?" "Be careful. Don't let your guard down. This Covid is serious shit! Promise me you'll take care of yourself and be safe." We each said, "I love you." I told him he'd come through this; it was only temporary so he could get stronger. I said I'd be BarkStrong, keep my faith, and continue praying. I reassured him I'd be there for Mom and both our families. Goodbye wasn't said. Our last words were, "Love ya, Sis." "Love ya too, Big Bro."

So few words, but such a huge blessing; I didn't have to carry the guilt of words left unspoken.

Although the phone chats and texts stopped, I continued to FaceTime my Big Bro as time allowed. He had some amazing ICU nurses who would periodically spare a few minutes and graciously hold the iPad so I could just talk to Duane in the days and months to come. I greatly appreciated being able to talk to him. Deep down, I know he heard me. But I still felt helpless.

Not able to be at the hospital, not able to help Duane and make him better, not able to physically give Pam, Brad, Brian, or Brittany a shoulder to lean on, literally not able to do a damn thing—I was helpless. That's a cruel, ruthless, and extremely harsh feeling for someone who thrives on helping others.

Fast-forward to October 6, 2020, when Pam called to tell me they had decided to turn off the ventilator the next day. I shared with you earlier the details of October 7, 2020. Again, helpless. There was no bottom to that deep pit; I just kept falling. Duane's passing was devastating. Not physically being with him at that moment was unbearable, bringing oppressive sadness and physical pain.

This was helplessness at its ultimate level for me. I had to watch my brother's last breath on a screen. Although that situation was beyond anyone's control, my inability to be there and hold his hand was excruciating. My sense of helplessness was amplified because I couldn't hold, hug, and comfort Pam, Brad, Brian, and Brittany. Adding to all of this, I was helpless in the ability to have Mom be with her son at the time of his death. Covid rules had control over the extenuating circumstances; I was literally left helpless and unable to do anything.

## *Reflections*

Is there something about the circumstances of your sibling's passing that left you feeling helpless? Do you currently feel helpless on your grief journey, like things are spinning out of control and there is nothing you can do to stop it or change it?

## Anger

Anger can come in a variety of ways, for a variety of reasons, and be directed toward a variety of people or circumstances. *My* anger wasn't toward God, as is sometimes the case. Instead, my anger was at Covid. How is it that Covid could dictate where I could and couldn't be? Here was this unknown "thing" that was taking over my brother's life and keeping me isolated from him. I was angry about a situation that I had absolutely no control over. I was only allowed to physically be at the hospital with Duane once during that three-month period. That momentous and heartfelt ninety-minute visit was the result of Pam pulling every string possible to get me, Mom, and my husband inside that ICU room. Thank you, Pam! I'll never forget Brian meeting us in the lobby with a hug and explaining to us how to act and respond once we got inside Duane's ICU room. At that moment, Brian let me know he, too, would always have my back. Once inside, Brittany's eyes met mine; the love between us didn't need to be spoken because it was something that was *felt between* us a million times—over and over. She stood right beside me as I lovingly talked to Duane, prayed over him, held his hand, and kissed his forehead. Amid the tremendous amount of love within that room, I was angry. Angry that Covid stipulations kept me from visiting him any other time. I was angry that I was not able to be there for Duane's last ventilated breath. Covid *sucks*! As a family, we all agreed to postpone Duane's celebration of life. Afterall, Covid was the reason we had to *have* a celebration of life anyway. Why would we want to jeopardize anyone else's health and well-being? Duane would have supported our decision wholeheartedly. Although I was 100 percent in support of the postponement, I was angry. Angry that our BarkStrong network, who had supported us for so long, wasn't able to be with us so we could all be comforted by one another.

Anger arose in me when dealing with people's insensitivity regarding their stance on Covid. Here we were in the midst of a pandemic, new territory for everyone, and people thought it would be best to debate Duane's previous health status with me and his family. It's at this point that I went into full Queen of Protection mode. Good Lord, my only sibling just died, and you want to "convince" me that he "*must* have had other extenuating health concerns"? We've all heard about not messing with Mama Bear; well, you don't mess with Sister Bear either! Let me set the record straight. There were *no* underlying circumstances! All those inconsiderate and inappropriate remarks brought out my intense need to defend Duane; the soft-spoken, quiet Kim disappeared.

> "The mildest, drowsiest sister has been known to turn
> tiger if her sibling is in trouble" (Clara Ortega).

What else stirred up anger in me? Certain comments made me angry. I totally understand that most people are at a loss for appropriate words to say when someone passes. Maybe it's because people feel the need to fill idle time with words; I'm not sure. I also know that for the most part that comments are not said with the intent to be hurtful or insensitive. However, it didn't help to hear, "He's in a better place." Yes, I *know* my Big Bro is in a better place; he's happy in heaven with his loved ones. But those words didn't make it better for me; they made me angry. "It's for the best" didn't sit kindly with me either. First of all, how does someone else know what's best for me, and if truth be told, the best would be that Duane was still here with me.

At times, I had anger toward all the future happenings that were stripped from me. These included the major events as well as the day-to-day phone conversations. It made me mad that Duane and I wouldn't be sharing our lives together anymore. We had plans for the future. We were hoping to retire at the same time so we could spend more time together. We had plans to go to Alaska together with our spouses in honor of my dad. The Alaskan trip was on Dad's bucket list. However, his dementia got the best of him, literally; that disease stripped my dad of everything. When Dad became Covid positive and passed away less than two months after Duane, every single reaction, response, and emotion piled on top of me like heavy boulders and buried me at the bottom of that grief pit.

I was also angry because from a societal standpoint, I was misunderstood as a sibling griever. Sympathies flow out to spouses, parents, and children (with no questions asked, *rightly so*); but for some reason, siblings are supposed to recover quickly and move on. What outsiders don't understand is that as siblings, we've had a lifetime of memories and significant connections that are ripped apart by the loss. As adult siblings, it's as if we are still children doing life together, no matter what our current age.

There was also anger as I didn't want to be *the only* one left to care for my aging mom (my dad was in the nursing home at this point). Duane and I had always promised each other we would do that phase of life together for our parents. We would be there *with* and *for* each other as we navigated through whatever life would throw our way as our parents aged. There were and still are many occasions and events that are happening, and I have to do them without my sidekick. And that makes me angry!

## *Reflections*

Has anger reared its ugly head for you, too? Take some time for yourself to reflect and process that anger. Don't be surprised or alarmed if anger periodically forces its way back into your thoughts in the days, months, and even years to come. If you're like me, it's bound to happen because you still have your whole future ahead of you without your sibling. My hope is that when anger does arise, you're able to recognize it for what it is and diffuse some of its debilitating power.

## Resourceless

I felt I had nowhere to turn. I knew only a few people, close to me, who had dealt with the death of a sibling, so that was one resource taken away and scratched off my list. I searched Amazon for grief books and ordered every book that looked as if it might be a helpful resource. There were very few books that were written specifically for sibling grief, and those that were didn't seem to deeply resonate with me. Where else could I turn for help? As I said, we were in the midst of a pandemic, and there were no such things as in-person grief support groups or in-person counseling. The wait lists for individual virtual counseling were months and years out. This situation stressed me out; there was an absence of means and methods to help me, and that brought more burdens. I was at a point where I knew I needed to find someone or something, yet I was batting zero at every turn, coming up empty. Eventually, I was connected with Megyn, a bereavement counselor at the hospital where Duane had spent three months in the ICU fighting Covid. (More about Megyn later in my turning point section.)

The following is an excerpt from *The Badass Within* (which was part of my Facebook post on 12/20/20 "BarkStrong by the Grace of God").

> "For months, I continued to say that my Big Bro would have a Testimony to share; he'd come out of it sharing how big his God was! Little did I know, at the time, that God had a different plan. "For I know the plans I have for you," says the LORD. "They are plans for good and not for disaster, to give you a future and a hope." (Jeremiah 29:11). God had a purpose for my pain and was preparing me to share my story of "test to testimony." Life has definitely thrown several back-to-back punches in the past months; punches that could certainly be considered knockouts."

So instead of being out for the count, why are Duane and Dad telling me to get back in the ring? Because they know I have a story to share—a story that might inspire someone to take that leap of faith and trust.

It's as if Duane and Dad were telling me, "It's time"; they had passed the torch to me, and it was now *my* time to carry that BarkStrong torch.

The following are more excerpts from *The Badass Within:*

> God is my source of strength; it is my faith and trust that allows me to get back up and step into the ring of life again. This doesn't mean I step back into the ring without bruises or without scars. It doesn't

mean I step back in without tears, sadness, or a heavy heart. What it does mean, however, is that I step back into the ring of life knowing I have a loving God who will never leave my side, no matter what fight or storms of life are ahead of me.

It was then and there that God tapped me and said, "Kim, when you're ready, you will write a book to provide a resource for others."

God continued to tap throughout my grief journey. (By the way, God keeps tapping until you listen.) I started out small by writing my chapter, "The Roller Coaster Ride of Grief" in *The Badass Within*. Although that was cathartic, I knew I wasn't done. God was still tapping and nudging me to write the book that I so desperately needed back in 2020.

> "If you don't see the book you want on the shelf, write it" (Beverly Cleary).

## *Reflections*

Do you feel like you have nowhere to turn? Are you searching for someone or something to be your lifeline? I pray that you find this book to be a helpful resource as you travel on your grief journey. Searching for a counselor is not a sign of weakness; it actually takes strength from within to reach out and ask for help along the way. I also pray you have found your own kind of BarkStrong network to support and guide you during this difficult time. I've started a grief support group in my area, and I pray you have something similar where you live. Connecting with people who are on a similar journey can be very helpful.

## Emptiness/Void

"Grief hurts. Nobody can replace a loved one who is no longer here, it's an emptiness that never goes away" (author unknown).

The more life experiences that Duane and I shared, and the more time we spent together, the more that seemed to be missing after he passed. I felt lost; it felt as though I was walking around aimlessly in the wilderness. I felt as if *my* life were gone too, like it had been siphoned right out of me. Although I had my family and a lot of friends who were amazing at loving and supporting me, life just felt meaningless. I had spent my life being a Lil Sis, and just like that, it was gone. My heart and physical world had a vacancy, and there was absolutely nobody who could fill it, not a single soul.

"This hole in my heart is in the shape of YOU. No one else can fit it. Why would I want them to?" (Jeanette Winterson).

Void – noun (voyd) – a completely empty space.

I am left with a void. There is the obvious physical void in which my Big Bro is no longer here on earth. I have a hole left in my being that's the shape of Duane. Part of my identity is gone; the youngest child space is empty. There is also the void in the loss of history; bonds were shattered, and our history will forever have a void that can't be filled. When a sibling dies, that piece of your childhood together goes too. There is the empty space for all future events and occasions where they should be sitting. For me, from this point forward, all significant events will be bittersweet, joyous times surrounded by the void of Duane and Dad's absence.

All the ill effects of my grieving were compounded exponentially. I was floundering around in my crater-sized grief pit, trying to figure out life without Duane in it, and less than two months later, I was faced with the devastation of my dad's death as well. Not only did I have the three-month-long emotional roller coaster ride with Duane's covid ordeal, but my emotions had been played with and tugged on for several years prior, as I had to watch my dad, my hero, succumb to dementia.

The following is an excerpt from *The Badass Within*:

As time passed, I slowly watched my dad, my hero, become someone I didn't know. From his standpoint, I was becoming someone he no longer recognized either. Two-sided verbal conversations eventually turned into one-sided conversations. Eyes that were once filled with life and stories became eyes with blank stares. His memory faded, but the power of touch didn't. Unspoken love remained. Unfortunately, the grieving process with dementia lingers while your loved one is still alive. That sucks! The longest goodbye kind of grief never really allows you time to catch your breath before the next twist, turn, or freefall comes.

When Dad passed away in December of 2020, I had to grieve for him a second time.

I had been grieving in slow motion for who my dad used to be before I ever lost my Big Bro. During all the stages of Dad's dementia, Duane and I still had each other to lean on. But now, my Big Bro was gone and my dad was gone, and there was absolutely no one who could, or ever would, be able to fill their shoes. I am left with a double vacancy in my heart, and my go-to guy isn't here to help me through it—no sibling, no Big Bro to grieve with for the loss of Dad.

> "Where you used to be, there is a hole in the world, which I find myself constantly walking around in the daytime, and falling into at night. I miss you like hell" (Edna St. Vincent Millay).

## *Reflections*

Are you experiencing an intense hollowness? I can confirm that sense of being. Your emptiness is real, and there is no one who can fill that specific vacancy for you. There is a new norm as you move forward, yet the hole will always be there. My sincere wish is that as time goes by, you begin to surround that empty space and envelope it with love, joy, peace, and hope. As you move forward, continue to protect the memories, stories, and true essence of your sibling inside that sacred vacancy. The void is a harsh reality. And I'm so sorry.

## Loss

"A brother shares childhood memories and grown-up dreams" (fbfreestatye.blogspot.com).

There is the loss of history. My husband, my kids, my grandkids, my extended family, or any of my friends don't have this common history with me; I am now the sole keeper of *my* history. And so, I clutch *my* history book snugly to my chest and breathe it into my heart—my autobiography of days gone by. There is the loss of the future; all future events and special occasions will forever be changed. Duane won't physically be a part of the celebrations. Dad won't physically be a part of the celebrations. It's hard to make new and happy memories without my two Bark men. The loss of a soul bond is indescribable to an outsider. It's a connection that runs so deep that it's unfathomable to anyone else's understanding. Duane was essential in my life. He was closer to me than anyone else. My Big Bro saw me in a profound sense. The loss of our friendship is still disabling at times. A true friend stands up for you no matter what. That person protects you emotionally and physically, making sure you're safe. Duane defended me anytime, anywhere. "I got your back, Sis."

It's this kind of loss that cannot be replaced. The loss of our family bond has been ripped to shreds, destroying the intactness of our original nucleus of four. I'm still trying to figure out how to step up and step into the roles Duane and Dad each played within our family unit. Fifty percent of a family of four seems like an enormous gap, a loss too great to wrap my head and heart around. The possibility of the impending loss of time spent together with Duane's family in the future leaves me disheartened. Will we remain intact as a BarkStrong family unit in the years to come, or will time take its toll, and, one by one, I'll have to suffer the loss of each of them as they move forward with their lives?

> "The loss is immeasurable but so is the love
> left behind" (author unknown).

## Reflections

Are you also feeling the immeasurable loss of so many things—the past, the present, and the future? I recognize that it's not just the physical loss of your sibling. It's so much more. Please offer yourself grace as you sort through the various losses. Know that this sense of loss can spring up at any given time and fiercely grab ahold of you. Remember that grief doesn't fit in a nice, tidy container; instead, there are times when it's more like a million pieces of confetti thrown into the air and freefalling all around you.

## Fear

Panic and fear set in. I was afraid of being alone for the rest of my life. I didn't know how I'd be able to do life without my brother. We were supposed to be a package deal. I was terrified by the reality of not having my source of strength, my level-headed decision-maker, or my go-to guy for all the years yet to come. Dealing with whatever comes my way as mom's elderly years play out is one of the biggest fears I have. Doing this stage of mom's life without my brother scares the living daylights out of me.

Another intense fear I had was with Covid. After his cruel and nightmarish three-month Covid battle, Duane departed from earth. During those months, we all listened as doctors told us time and again there was nothing more they could do. We watched as miracles would happen, and the doctors were flabbergasted as to how he could possibly be responding while on a ventilator and in a medically induced coma. We rode this horrific roller-coaster ride of hope-filled highs and devastating lows from July until October. "Please don't let me have to deal with Covid again," I prayed; actually I begged. Dad, who was in a nursing home with dementia, tested Covid positive about six weeks after Duane's passing. Unfortunately, Dad didn't make it either, as he succumbed to the combination of Covid's ill effects and dementia. The fear in me was intensified; was it something in our gene pool? So when I got Covid, landed in the ER, was terribly sick, and needed an infusion, I was petrified. Would Covid have the final say for me too? I lived in fear wondering who Covid would take from me next.

Yet another fear I had was the fear of death. It wasn't that I was afraid of dying, and it really wasn't me being afraid of other loved ones dying—although that's obviously not something I'm delighted to think about. Instead, it was the fear of me *being* and *living* (and I use those terms lightly) in that mental and physical place of despair and desolation ever again. I knew that the death of a loved one is what took me into that deep, dark pit, and I was petrified of even the thought of ever reliving that experience again.

## *Reflections*

Are you facing fears that have left you feeling paralyzed? What is it that brings great panic and anxiety to you? Whatever it is, address it. From your perspective, it's real, valid, and certainly not anything to be pushed under a rug.

## Guilt

Guilt raised its ugly head several times. At first, I carried the self-imposed guilt trip of not physically being there. During these traumatic three months, I wanted nothing more than to be at that hospital holding Duane's hand, kissing his forehead, and talking to him. I wanted to be in that ICU room not only comforting Duane, but his wife and kids as well. You know that phrase, "I would have done anything…"; that was me.

As if that guilt weren't enough, I felt the immense heaviness and guilt of not physically being there when Duane passed. Who does that? What kind of Sis are you if you can't be there when it means the most? Even though I knew I couldn't be there, my heart didn't agree. I beat myself up over this for quite some time, all the while knowing the Covid stipulations were beyond my control. Again, my heart and head were disconnected, and guilt took over. Eventually, I found it best to offer myself grace; there was nothing I could have done to change that scenario. However, I lived with that guilt for some time.

Another kind of guilt I had was that of pushing people away. I had tremendous support from my loving family. Our massive BarkStrong network reached out in so many ways as well. Yet, I pushed everyone away. They witnessed my mental and physical deterioration and wanted to help me in any way possible; instead, I cocooned myself. I was sinking further into that bottomless pit. Countless people continued to offer me ropes, and I rejected their offers. It's like I was watching someone else play the leading role in my life's movie. I could see everyone who was relentlessly trying to help, and I knew I should grab hold of the ropes, yet I couldn't get myself to poke out of that miserable, desolate cocoon. Who pushes away loved ones and people who genuinely care and only want the best for you? What was wrong with me anyway? This guilt was a heavy load to carry. Thankfully, my family and friends never gave up on trying, never left my side, and ultimately showed me unconditional love at its finest!

I'm so thankful that I didn't have to carry the guilt of things left unsaid. Duane and I always spoke openly about our love for each other. "Love ya, Sis." "Love ya too, Big Bro." I'll hear those words vividly for the rest of my life—what a blessing.

## Reflections

Guilt is real and agonizingly uncomfortable. Are you carrying around guilt that needs to be released? Oftentimes, guilt is something we place on ourselves and clench tightly. Sit quietly with the guilt, surrendering what isn't yours to carry.

## Loneliness/Isolation

Dovetailing from the guilt is the sense of loneliness and isolation I felt. I created a self-imposed alienation. Looking back, it would have been much better for my overall well-being to not isolate myself, but at that time, I wasn't thinking with that type of clarity. At that time, I didn't want to be around people; I just wanted to be left alone to sulk, mope, not think, and certainly not have to face the reality and begin to process what had just happened. On some level, this was my denial. Another part of the loneliness was the reality of actually being alone. Duane and I did life together. I was left alone to continue my life without him. Every time I picked up my phone to call or text him to chat, I had to pause, remembering that he was no longer here, and I couldn't talk to him. When I had exciting news to share with him, I couldn't. When I had a question for him about my impending retirement, I couldn't ask. I realized over and over again that I was alone. Duane's passing left me feeling intense loneliness. Once again, intellectually I know that I have a loving and supportive family and my BarkStrong network is phenomenal; I'm surrounded by a huge support system. Yet there is a place in my heart that will forever be lonely—lonely for my brother.

## *Reflections*

Have you disengaged yourself? Have you chosen to disconnect from the outside world? I totally understand if you're wanting to isolate yourself. I get it. Maybe that's your form of denial too. However, there's a fine line between isolation that gives yourself time to process, and isolation that is prolonged extensively and begins to hinder your well-being. I pray you find the middle ground.

## Forgotten

"Most siblings will spend 80 percent to 100 percent of their lifetime with their siblings on this earth.... It is a really, really big deal to lose a sibling. Very significant, but it's very unacknowledged" (Dr. Heidi Horsley).

The death of a sibling is frequently the most neglected loss. The surviving sibling is often referred to as the "forgotten mourner." It wasn't my spouse, it wasn't my child, and it wasn't my parent; I was "just a sibling." It was hard for me when well-meaning people asked, "How's your mom?" "How's Pam?" "How are their kids?" Although those were all genuine and heartfelt questions (which most definitely deserved recognition and answers), I always anticipated the next question to be, "How are you doing?" More often than not, however, that question wasn't asked. I too was extremely concerned for Mom, Pam, Brad, Brian, and Brittany. It tore me apart to see their immense sadness. It sucks watching the people you love hurting. However, I longed for people to recognize my pain and sincerely inquire about my well-being as well.

"It's OK to feel like your loss is the worst loss in the world.
It is the worst loss in *your* world" (author unknown).

Note to self for future reference: be mindful of sibling grievers and ask how they are doing.

## *Reflections*

Do you feel as though you've been forgotten because you're "just a sibling"? Do you feel like the bystander who has no stake in this grieving process? Let me reiterate: all grief is real and is valid no matter who the griever is. I see your pain, and I can empathize.

## Physical and Emotional Erosion

When grief is hanging over you all the time like a dark cloud, it's hard to do anything. It's hard to concentrate, hard to care about anyone or anything, hard to be motivated to carry on with your normal life. And when you do attempt to and force yourself to do so, it takes all the energy you can muster up, leaving you exhausted. It's weird; I was exhausted to "just be," doing nothing, and I was also exhausted by attempting to do. Combine that with the fact my sleep pattern was all screwed up. I rarely got consistent hours of sleep. Even though I wasn't doing much, I still felt completely physically exhausted.

Grief left me emotionally exhausted as well. It felt like I couldn't get away from it. It lived inside me, and therefore I couldn't ever shake it. It was with me every second, minute, hour of the day. Something or someone would spark a memory of Duane, and that all-consuming, suck-the-energy-from-you kind of exhaustion depleted me like a pin poking a balloon.

Physically and emotionally, my health plummeted during Duane's ICU stay and intensified in the months that followed his passing. In the midst of trying to figure out life without Duane, I was gut punched again, in late November, when Dad tested positive for Covid while in the nursing home with dementia. In early December, Dad passed away, less than two months after Duane. My grief suitcase, packed with all its emotions and side effects, was compounded exponentially, busting at the seams, and spilling out all the contents once again. The two men who were my world, my everything, since birth were gone, just like that. I hadn't even begun to climb up out of the grief pit, and gale force winds tossed me around at the bottom like a toothpick in the wind, having just enough power to lift me ever so slightly and then hurl me back to the ground, slamming me with a breathtaking force. How can life knock you down twice when you haven't even been able to stumble to your feet from the first blow? On the outside, I looked vaguely familiar to others. I had lost a lot of weight and was weighing what I had weighed in middle school. When my son saw me for the first time in months, I had obviously caught him off guard. "Mom, you're scaring the shit out of me." I was losing my hair as a result of the extreme stress. My body was reacting adversely to the reality of my immense and intense grief of losing the two men in my life who were *always* there (in every sense of the word) for me from the moment I was born. They were the two men who had loved me, BarkStrong, every day for fifty-nine years. My lifelong relationships with these two men are the foundation of who I am today and are the reason I can love so fiercely.

On the inside I was crumbling; the old Kim had disappeared. Emotionally, I was shut down. From September through December I was rarely at work. I was tied to my phone, waiting for life-altering news; I put my life on hold. I had no desire to teach, no desire to be around people. My students didn't need the "me" I had become. They deserved better than what I currently was. For some reason, I felt that if I had a word to describe the intensity of what was happening to me, I'd be able to validate it for myself. "Sad" was way too generic, way too shallow, and definitely didn't describe the impact or depth of my ill-being. A Google search led me to *anhedonia*, the loss of interest in previously rewarding or enjoyable activities. Now there's an interesting word to describe an emotional shutdown!

By late December, the by-products of my double grief had taken its toll, and I was riding in the back of an ambulance to a hospital eighty miles away with stroke-like symptoms. My body was doing some crazy things the longer my stress lingered. It was so much more than "fight or flight"; it was all-consuming, day-in, day-out, 24/7. I couldn't continue on the destructive path I was on; something had to change.

The following is an excerpt from *The Badass Within:*

I took a leave of absence from work in January, and spent my days sleeping, praying, talking to my bereavement counselor and reading every book on grief I could find, [all in hopes that by the end of the month, I'd physically and emotionally be in a better place]. In February, I went back to teaching. That was short-lived when I got Covid. Extremely sick and needing an infusion, I wondered, *will Covid kill me too?* Life had knocked me down for eight grueling months. *Is there seriously no bottom to this pit?* Beaten down and broken, it seemed impossible to get up. *Who could possibly take me from emptiness to wanting to enjoy life again at its fullest?*

## Reflections

Are you noticing the ill effects of physical changes? Perhaps you're in the trenches so deep that you haven't noticed. I urge you to listen to those who are voicing their worry out of love, care, and concern. Sometimes, they can see more clearly than you can while you're in the midst of your grieving. Are you experiencing emotional erosion? I get it; it sucks, and emotionally you're probably drained, exhausted, and in the depths of despair. Hindsight is eye-opening, and it allows me to advise you to reach out to others and seek help because prolonged time, cocooned in a shell, can be detrimental to your physical, emotional, mental, and spiritual well-being.

## Identity/Role Changes, Lost Identity

"Our family chain is broken and nothing seems the same, but as God calls us one by one the chain will link again" (Ron Trammer).

We had a family system. There were norms, roles, traditions, and patterns for each of us individually. Yet, as a unit, we were one cohesive, BarkStrong family. Each of us had our place within the family unit, keeping us balanced and functioning relatively smoothly. Duane's death presented me (and Mom) with figuring out how to juggle new identities and roles. When Dad passed away less than two months later, our family was off balance times two. For Mom and me, that was 50 percent altered within our family. Our family dynamics had changed drastically. I was no longer a Sis, or was I? I was no longer the baby of the family; I immediately went from youngest to the oldest in a matter of minutes. I immediately became an only child. Do not pass go, do not collect $200. Duane and I had specific characteristics that complimented each other. Now, I'm left behind to redefine my identity. I needed to readjust and reorganize my roles. I find that I've taken on some of Duane's characteristics as I've stepped into his roles.

I went from the youngest child to the oldest and, at the same time, the only child. This left me frustrated, helpless, and fearful. Our characteristics supported each other, and when one dies (in my case, two deaths) those strengths need to be picked up by those left behind.

Duane was my best friend, not just my brother. We were in sync so much that we could finish each other's sentences, and when one phone was pinging with a text notification, so was the other's because a call or text was coming through. I looked up to both Dad and Duane as my role models, with so much love and respect.

## *Reflections*

Your identity has changed as well, no matter where you fell in line as a sibling. And because of that, your role within the family will undoubtedly change as well. Are you finding that your family system of operation is off balance? Are you trying to figure out how to navigate the new dynamics? Redefining, reorganizing, and readjusting can be painstaking and confusing. The new norm takes time; be gentle with yourself as you adjust and make sense of it.

## DOES SOMEONE HAVE A HOW-TO MANUAL, PLEASE?

There will never be a how-to manual for maneuvering through grief. There are, however, commonalities as we navigate our new norm.

Your emotions, stresses, worries, reactions, responses, and feelings probably don't match mine exactly; my guess is, however, that there are similarities. It might be the same types of emotions mirrored but felt in ways that are deeply personal to you. These don't necessarily happen in order, and you're usually experiencing more than one at a time. Remember, it's OK to not be OK.

# I'M BEGGING YOU, PLEASE LET US HELP YOU

**MY HUSBAND AND OUR THREE ADULT CHILDREN** were beside themselves. For months, they had watched my physical and emotional decline. They threw me countless ropes to raise me out of that grief pit, and I refused to grab hold of any of them. Our children all had families and lives of their own yet were insistent on helping me to get better. As I said, I lived an all-consuming life that completely revolved around Duane's ups and downs while in the ICU. I was attached to my phone, and I would drop everything (or anyone) when texts and phone calls came in. As if in slow motion, they watched their wife/mom fade away. In their eyes, it seemed as though I had abandoned both of those two roles. Sadly, my actions were verifying what they were feeling. I *was* dropping the ball. I didn't consciously choose to wash my hands of being a wife or mom; however, the reality was that those two roles were on the back burner. I fell short. I let them down and hurt them in the process. To this day, that part of my grieving process brings me enormous sadness and regret because there is nothing in this world I love more than being a wife, mom, and grandma.

They tried to be gentle, they tried to be discreet, and finally they had no other choice but to give me some tough love. My husband Al, and our kids (JJ, Brianna, and Lucas) laid it on the line and told me how they felt. If my days and nights were consumed with Duane, that left zero time for them. That stung. That hurt. What a reality check. Were they right? Was I really giving *all* my time and energy to Duane? Was I so consumed with the things I couldn't control about Duane's deteriorating health and eventual death that I had lost sight of *my* family and all that they were doing to help me through? It was time for a family meeting. I wrote a letter to Al and each of our kids, asking our kids to come home for a family meeting. Spouses, significant others, and our grandkids weren't included; this was something *our* family had to address head on. Right there in my living room, we had a heart-to-heart. Each of us had an opportunity to voice our cares and concerns without judgment. It was real. It was raw. It was authentically us. Tears, hugs, words, and unconditional love spewed out like hot lava oozing its way down a volcano. In the end, I was better able to understand their perspective, and they were better able to understand my frame of mind as well. This was a catalyst for us as a family to move forward in the midst of my despair and desperation. The road ahead of us was long and full of curves and sharp corners, as I was still in the pit, but bottom line, we each knew we weren't giving up on each other. (BarkStrong being lived out in the Allen and Kim White family.) My husband was fantastic. He tried as hard as he could to console me and help me get through the worst year of my life. He supported me in every possible way he could think of. He made every effort to understand where I was coming from, but nobody gave him a manual for how to deal with a grieving spouse. Grief had taken over the wife he once knew. He too felt helpless; everything he was trying wasn't bringing me out of that deep, dark place. Try as he might, I wasn't responding. They say that when devastating situations arise, a marriage is tested. You either come out of it stronger or you throw in the towel. Fortunately, my husband and I weathered that horrendous and all-consuming storm of life. He's been there for me and continues to be by my side, supporting me, cheering me on, and, more importantly, holding me tight when the intense sadness resurfaces, washing over me like an unexpected ocean tide that disintegrates the beautiful sandcastles in its path.

My kids were phenomenal at trying to help me get through that devastating and destructive time in my life as well. They showed me time and time again unconditional love and what it means to be BarkStrong. As adults, they each had their own lives and families to take care of, yet their concern and support for me never failed or faltered. I knew without a shadow of a doubt that they had my back and would help me fight the fight until I once again was the mom they knew (or at least the mom that was very similar to the mom they knew).

At the time, my grandkids ranged in age from two to fifteen. Without knowing the full extent of my despair, yet knowing "grandma wasn't acting the same," they also tried to throw me ropes. They drew me pictures, wrote me notes, hugged me tight, tried to get me involved in their lives and activities, told me they loved me, and spent time snuggled on my lap. As hard as they tried, I couldn't snap out of it. I knew, however, that they would keep pouring their unconditional love into me. "Love you. Always and forever. No matter what" is a phrase that we not only say, but live.

Although Mom and I were each grieving the same person, we each grieved (and continue to grieve) in very different ways. Plain and simple, neither of us is right, and neither of us is wrong. However, as we all know, there is nothing plain or simple when it comes to grief. I know Mom was worried, concerned, and distressed watching me wallow around for days, weeks, and months on end. After all, we needed each other; our nucleus was down to 50 percent, and I was slipping away. Although she too wanted to come to my rescue and make it all better (as mothers do), I remained in my cocoon. Mom's BarkStrong ways continued to glimmer throughout; it's something you do, it's how you act, it's how you love. It was the unspoken, unwritten concept that encompassed always having each other's back, always being there for each other, always supporting each other, always sticking up for each other, and always loving each other unconditionally. Mom didn't give up on me; that wasn't a thought that crossed her mind.

Duane's family was, and continues to be, another great source of my personal strength. Just like there's no manual for how to grieve, there is no manual for how grievers should help each other in the midst of the most horrendous times of their lives.

As a wife, Pam needed to grieve in her own way, processing the loss of her husband. As a sibling, my grieving didn't mirror her ways, but our ways were reflective of each other—we both lost someone who was our world. We both tried to help each other while floundering daily. Bottom line is that there was an unwritten given; we weren't going to give up until the other had grabbed the life vest.

Brittany and I talked multiple times a week, sometimes multiple times a day. I knew, full well, that I was in a dark pit. Although I wasn't in a good frame of mind, I was completely aware that she was devastated as well; after all, this was her dad, and she too was a daddy's girl. Together, we muddled around in that mess. Although we had an arduous time helping ourselves, we had an unspoken code that we were in this together. If we fell, we fell together; if one of us saw a glimmer of hope, we tried to be the Bic flame for the other. Although there were plenty of times I was unable to think clearly, I innately knew that together, we would somehow survive, never giving up on each other.

My nephews, Brad and Brian, went a little more inward, so to speak. They were supportive of me, but we didn't talk as regularly. Brian reassured me from the get-go that he would pick up where Duane left off. He told me he'd heard Duane say many times throughout the years, "I've got your back, Sis." Brian let me know that no matter what, he'd always have my back and be there for me. Brad, too, let me know that he's always here for me. Brian, Brad, and I "did grief" differently than Pam, Brittany, and I did. Even though we didn't talk to each other as much, we knew the unspoken essence of

## I'M BEGGING YOU, PLEASE LET US HELP YOU

BarkStrong—always there, always having each other's back, always supportive, and loving unconditionally.

My friends were, and still are, the best people in the world; I like to call them my BarkStrong network. They reached out to me in countless ways; whether it was phone calls, texts, voicemails, gifts, flowers, or food, they let me know that they were not leaving my side. Unfortunately, I did my best to push them away, too, but they never gave up on me. They were relentless, continuing to be true and loyal to our friendships. *Persistent* describes it best, as they found multiple ways of reaching out and trying to tap into the Kim they knew and loved.

Everyone tried. No one gave up. Thank goodness they all stayed by my side even when I pushed them away.

# FORK IN THE ROAD

**AT FIRST, I WAS OBLIVIOUS** to knowing or wanting anything different; sloshing around in that pit felt comfortable. It was in that space of yuck that I didn't have to push myself into being or behaving in a different way. For all intents and purposes, that was *my* norm, and in some regards, I was OK with that. That hole had become my new residency. It was stagnant, yet comfortable, sad to say, but *that place* was my comfort zone. My whole outer world was intensely changing, fluctuating, shifting all so quickly, and part of me didn't want to find out what life entailed outside of that box. I didn't want to face the realities of dealing with the unknown of my new norm.

My bereavement counselor, Megyn, was truly a godsend. It was during our weekly phone conversations that she provided me with a safe haven to say what I was feeling, cry when I couldn't contain it, and sit silently when I had no words available. With the utmost of compassion and the sincerest empathy, Megyn sat with me week after week, gradually, and ever so gently guiding and supporting me as I worked through layer upon layer of my grief-stricken self. I distinctly remember the day that I had a breakthrough while talking with Megyn. I was dressed in my typical, bottom-of-the-pit attire of black yoga pants and a hooded Lancaster sweatshirt. I was sitting in the tan leather recliner in my living room, when Megyn's phone call came through. Our session began as it always did. "Hi Kim, it's Megyn." We were about fifteen minutes into our hour-long session when I told Megyn that I was longing for peace and joy back in my life, but I didn't know how to go about it. First of all, I didn't know if it was possible, and second, I had no idea what that would even look like. Would some version of the old Kim really be able to resurface and move forward? As we continued our chat, Megyn talked about post-traumatic growth. I had never heard that term before.

> *Post-traumatic growth is the positive psychological change that some individuals experience after a life crisis or traumatic event. Post-traumatic growth doesn't deny deep distress, but rather posits that adversity can unintentionally yield changes in understanding oneself, others, and the world.* (Psychology Today. https://www.psychologytoday.com/us/basics/post-traumatic-growth.)

Megyn explained the difference between post-traumatic depreciation (PTD) and post-traumatic growth (PTG). PTD and PTG can be defined, respectively, as negative and positive changes in the aftermath of trauma. Megyn clarified these two with the following metaphor. "Kim, you've been given a pile of rocks. What do you want to do with them? You can sit amongst them and get buried by them, or you can mold them, shape them, and paint them, creating something beautiful. Kim, what do you want to come from this devastating situation you've been dealt?" That moment was my fork in the road. It was time. Time to make a decision. Would I be content buried in the pile of rocks, missing out on what life had in store for me? (I was finally beginning to realize that I didn't want to live the rest of my life *that* way.) Or did I want to get back into the ring of life and move forward with my family, friends, and all that life had to offer?

At the fork, I chose a narrow path to the right (pun intended, it was the *right* path for me). I wanted joy. I wanted peace. I wanted hope. I wanted to *live* again! But who could possibly take me from emptiness to wanting to enjoy life again at its fullest? I knew it wouldn't be easy, and I knew it would take time, but with intention, I *would* move forward (which is way different from "move on," in my opinion), appreciating life and all its possibilities. Moving from despair to deliberate and intentional hope felt good. It felt right. As I said, God keeps tapping until you listen! I know without a shadow of a doubt that it was God's grace that brought me through. He was busy orchestrating the details all along, placing people and opportunities in my life, showing up with His divine timing.

> "Let God turn your pain into purpose, your grief into growth" (Diana C. Derringer).

Although faith has always been an important part of my life, there were times during the messiness of Duane's ordeal that I felt myself faltering. I tried so hard to keep God close to me, but that seemed to be fading too, just like my Big Bro's health. The truth is, God doesn't falter. God doesn't back away. And God doesn't give up on people. He certainly didn't give up on me.

The following is an excerpt from *The Badass Within:*

Walk closer, Kim. You're not alone. I'll never leave you. I'm right here in the eye of your storm.

The most devastating year of my life was 2020. Fifty percent of my nucleus family was taken from me in less than two months. All along, God had a purpose for my pain and was preparing me to share my story with others. God was making me stronger in my faith so I *could* share it with others. God was placing people in my life, so when I was ready, I would make a difference for others' grief journeys. God provided me with *everything* I needed at *exactly* the right time. God needed me and my story to show others what faith is all about. "Your ministry is found where you've been broken. Your testimony is where you've been restored" (author unknown).

God was saying, "Kim, do more than talk the talk. Walk more fully in your walk. Tell people, "I was here, a broken soul, and now I'm telling my story with God by my side." My family and friends couldn't pull me out of that deep hole, *I* couldn't even will myself out; it was God's grace that allowed me to rise above my brokenness.

> "The final stage of healing is using what happens to you to help other people" (Gloria Steinem).

## Reflection

Do you feel as though you're coming to *your* fork in the road (or at least have the hopes of *someday* coming to that fork)? Are you wanting something different because your current state of stagnation and sluggishness isn't your vision for your future life? It'll take courage, intentional work, and deliberate effort, but I promise you it will be worth it. Remember, it's not *moving on* without your sibling, it's *moving forward*, all the while growing and learning along the way. As you reflect on the emotional and physical devastation you've been going through after losing your sibling, I pray that as time goes on, you begin to experience a sense of peace and joy in your life because you've intentionally *chosen* to do so. When that happens, and it will, please use *your* healing process to reach out and help others who are stumbling and staggering through their grief journey. It takes a fellow griever to know. Sibling grievers are an entity in and of ourselves; we need each other.

## Glimpses of Light

I wanted to come out of this on the other side and someday be able to help others. I knew in my gut that someday my pain would have purpose and my test would become a testimony. I would utilize my growth after trauma, share my grief story, and pray that I might be the lighthouse, a beacon of light, for others who are floundering in a grief-stricken, dark place.

I had a burning in my heart and gut. It was a newfound purpose and passion to help others find hope, joy, and peace, even though, even if, and even when. I want others to experience joy without the guilt of being happy, just like I've experienced.

I can only speak for myself; God is my foundation.

The following is an excerpt from *The Badass Within*.

My one constant was God. I prayed for hope, joy and peace to return to my life. Before this happened, I had faith, but wasn't growing in my faith or sharing it with others. I was sitting in junkyard tires filled with slimy, stagnant water. God used 2020 to dump out the sludge water and refill me with His living water. I've been growing in my faith, and now I'm doing what God placed in my heart. I'm sharing it with others by sharing my story. If it can help others walk closer to God as they journey through grief, then my pain was not in vain.

My mission is to be a candle for you, providing a source of light. If you so choose, allow me to be the lighthouse in your darkness.

Dad and Duane spent their lives influencing others and leaving an imprint. In my opinion, they left a legacy. I've decided to pick up their BarkStrong torch that they've passed to me and carry on for them, making certain I also have an impact, influence others, and leave an imprint on those whom I encounter on my path.

To honor these two amazing BarkStrong men and keep their memories and legacies alive, I'm insistent on using my story for good. This book is a product of doing just that. Besides being an author, I started a grief support group for the communities around me, where I act as the group's facilitator. I offer family grief support through my business, Mindful Empowerment. I'm adamant about sharing my grief story on whatever platform necessary to help others. It is my joy and honor to talk about the essence of who we were together—my relationships with both Dad and Duane—to share stories and say their names.

The following is excerpted from *The Badass Within*.

Although I miss the essence of us, I've found that part of accepting the loss of these two incredible men includes honoring Duane and Dad daily.

> "Be the things you loved most about the people who are gone" (author unknown).

Although I can't hike *your* grief walk for you, as that is your personal journey, I can tell you that it's OK to find joy again, and I pray that you will. It's OK to experience happiness; you'll catch yourself smiling and realize there is no longer guilt attached for doing so. You'll welcome a sense of peace that has been hidden for so long. Sooner or later, you'll be willing to inch your way forward, appreciating life and all the possibilities that lie ahead. You will find yourself creating new ways to honor the legacy of your sibling who's gone.

There are times when I slip back into old patterns. I recognize I need to get out of my head, own and honor my grief for what it is, and allow the rest of my BarkStrong family to do the same. None of us are walking an identical path on our grief journey, and that's OK. I don't need to beat myself up wondering if I'm doing it right.

Here are some ideas that you might find helpful as you pursue the glimpses of light within your darkness. The following are suggestions as you move forward on your journey. They were what I found to be helpful. Take what resonates with you, and implement them into your life; feel free to set the rest aside.

**God/Religion.** Explore your spirituality, pray, listen to Christian music, read devotionals, meet with your pastor or priest, connect with others who are strong in their faith and can mentor you along the way. I am amazed at how my faith journey has grown because of and since this tragedy in my life. I couldn't do this on my own; it's clear to me that God carried me through the storm.

> "Let God turn your pain into purpose, your grief into growth" (Diana C. Derringer).

**Writing/Journaling.** Journal your thoughts and emotions, journal your memories of you and your sibling, write a letter to your sibling. I've found, looking back through my journals, that I can literally see the gradual changes and shifting of my mindset. It was during the last three years that I've rekindled my love of writing. I've always enjoyed writing but didn't pursue it, so to speak. This is my third book that has been published. The first book I wrote a chapter in was *The Badass Within*. My chapter, "The Roller Coaster Ride of Grief," tells my personal journey during and after Duane's passing.

For the second book, *Graceful Growth,* I was co-lead author and wrote the chapter "Double Elimination Squared." It describes the connection I had with my dad, giving readers a glimpse of the daddy's little girl who had to lose her dad, not once, but twice (his mind to Alzheimer's and his body to Covid complications).

And here I am writing again, as you have this book in your hand—my first solo book.

Whether it's writing a few sentences at a time in a journal, being a part of a book collaboration, or hammering out your own book, maybe writing is a form of personal therapy for you.

**Physical activity.** Do yoga, go for walks, lift weights, begin to revisit activities you used to enjoy, or perhaps now is the time to take up a new physical activity; the possibilities are endless. When I am outside in nature, I'm able to get grounded and reset. Going for a walk, whether it be a power walk or a slow stroll, allows me to feel the fresh air, feel the sun's warmth on my face, and be mindful of my surroundings; nature has a way that often refreshes my outlook on the day.

**Meditation.** There are a wide variety of apps (Headspace, Calm, The Mindfulness App, Breathe, Insight Timer, Expand: Beyond Meditation, etc.), and there is also a wealth of guided meditations on YouTube. I have created several guided meditations that I use at the beginning of the classes I teach. You don't have to be perfect at meditating; that defeats the purpose. Instead, just be willing to practice it consistently; there's a reason it's called a meditation *practice*, not meditation *perfect*.

**Mindfulness practices.** The essence of mindfulness is paying attention, on purpose, in the moment. Mindfulness is all about training our brains to be in the moment, by focusing on our breath. I like to say, "Be present where your feet are." Mindfulness practices allow us to notice/be aware of and feel the current emotions for what they are in the moment. However, when we concern ourselves with the what-ifs, the should haves, and the could haves, we are robbing ourselves of the present moment. It is physically impossible to live in two places at once; therefore, we must choose where to live—the past, present, or future. For me, practicing mindfulness is now second nature. There are so many benefits to being mindful that I teach these techniques and practices to kids, teens, and adults in my business, Mindful Empowerment.

**Gratitude practice.** Make it a point daily to intentionally search for reasons to be grateful and thankful. It may be as simple as having gratitude for a soft pillow to rest your head upon at night. Gratitude is a wonderful cyclic event—the more you practice gratitude, the more things you recognize to be grateful for. I like to bookend my days with gratitude. Before my feet hit the floor in the morning, I give a gratitude, and when my head hits the pillow at night, I offer another gratitude. In doing the "bookend" method of gratitude, I am sure to get a minimum of two gratitudes per day. This, too, has become second nature for me. I find myself intentionally looking for other gratitudes throughout my days. Gratitude practices have helped me to live in a happier state of being. Even on my awful days, I am able to find people or things to be thankful for.

**Self-care.** Eat, sleep, hydrate, be active, get outside, enjoy the sunlight, enjoy a massage, get a manicure, take a warm bath. Again, the possibilities are endless; do the things that make your soul happy. I invite you to sit, be still, and go within; do some personal reflecting. What is it that makes your soul happy? Once you have that list, pencil some of those things into your calendar. Be intentional about carving out time for yourself. It may sound cliché, but you cannot pour from an empty cup; if your cup is bone dry, you cannot give yourself the love and care you need, and you can't give anything to those around you either. Over time, your self-care will probably change. In the beginning of my grief journey, sleep was probably my #1 type of self-care, followed by warm baths. Both of these could be done without having to be around anyone else. As I've moved forward in my grief journey, I've added back other types of self-care that I used to enjoy. I'm actually able to enjoy doing things that involve others now.

**Allow emotions and tears.** Allow yourself to feel emotions; they come and go like clouds in the sky or waves in the ocean. Emotions continue to rise, crest, and recede all day long. Tears are cleansing and healing; God "hears" tears when words won't come. For me, the anniversary days and the firsts (for example, the first Christmas without him) brought a ton of emotions and tears. Please be aware that the emotions and tears don't just come during specified days and times; that's OK, and it's not uncommon. There are many random days/moments that I am still overcome with the rawness of the reality and the roller coaster of emotions that burst in like a stranger entering my home without knocking, interrupting and intruding on my okayness. I find myself crying for no apparent reason.

**Welcome/accept the support of others.** Find your network of friends and/or family. Slowly be willing to allow the possibility of being around them again. Hindsight is 20/20 for this one! Thank goodness my people were relentless. If you are currently keeping your people at bay, I hope they're the best of the best like my BarkStrong network is. I get it. I understand. It's a process. It takes time. However, I strongly encourage you to take baby steps toward allowing others to support you, even if that means they sit and hold your hand without talking. Human touch is absolutely vital.

**Seek guidance.** Set up counseling services, meet with a pastor, ask for help. *Your* people *want* to help you; go ahead, it's OK. Connect with people—family, friends, a support network, social media sibling grief groups, etc. Connecting with others isn't a sign of weakness; it takes great strength to surrender to "I can't do this alone." I know this can be a fine line for some; only you know when enough is enough.

**Share stories.** Keep the memories of your sibling alive by sharing stories. For me, this brings a sense of peacefulness, calm, and comfort. I love sharing with others the stories about Duane and me. I like to let others know just who we were as a duo, as well as who he was as a man.

**Say their name.** Tell others it's OK to say their name as well; in fact, it's more than OK! Yes, you might actually have to give them permission to say your sibling's name. Oftentimes, people don't know what to do. They think it will hurt you and make you sadder if they mention your sibling's name. In reality, when we don't hear our sibling's name, we begin to think that others have forgotten about them. I find myself perking up as soon as I hear, "Duane." I look forward to hearing what's going to be said after that.

**Create.** Create photo albums. Find those special pictures of your sibling and frame them. Create a memory book or scrapbook. Create ways to keep your sibling's memories alive. I have been gifted several framed pictures of

Duane and me. They hang prominently in my dining room. Not only do I see them every time I walk through the room, but others see them as well when we're entertaining at our home. Many times, these pictures are ice breakers for conversations about Duane. Yes, say his name, ask me questions. Heck, I can even tell you stories if you'd like!

**Ask.** Ask others to share their memories of your sibling and have them write the memories down for you. You'll have a treasured collection of additional memories to have as a keepsake. I thought I knew most stories about Duane, but the exciting reality was that there were many other stories I had never heard before. My nephews and niece have reached out several times to ask me to tell them stories and memories from days gone by. This is a way that I can help make sure Duane's life carries on for not only his children, but also his grandchildren.

**Honor them.** Perhaps on your sibling's birthday, or his/her "angelversary," start an annual memorial event: plant a tree, think of unique ways you can honor your sibling. Thanks to a brilliant idea that Duane's kids had, our family has implemented an annual Duane Bark Educational Fund Memorial Golf Outing. We raise money for educational scholarships while enjoying one of Duane's many favorite sports.

**Take a day at a time.** Remember, it's a grief *journey*; you will forever be traveling from the place of "before this happened" to "after this happened." It takes time. Sometimes you can do a day at a time, and sometimes it's literally all you can do to get through moment by moment. Offer yourself grace. It's OK. As a grief facilitator, I cannot stress this enough. Allow yourself grace, time, and compassion. Please know that some days you'll feel like you're rocking it, and other days, you feel like the tsunami wave just slapped you around, leaving you to collapse under the rush of waves. It's during those times, especially, that you can do some mindfulness practices and just be in that moment—literally telling yourself, "I can conquer five more minutes." There will be times where you resort to moment by moment living, and there will be times where you can be at a place where you can function from day to day. Whatever the pace, it is OK. It is *your* journey.

**Set aside grief time.** Some people have found it valuable to allot yourself grief time, giving yourself a specific time to grieve, and then doing something else when the allotted time is up. This didn't work for me, but perhaps it is something that resonates with you.

**Listen to music.** Find your favorite genres of music and create playlists. Some people find music to be therapeutic. I've always been drawn to music, so this was beneficial for me. I've had people in our grief support group share their grief playlists with each other. They say that some of the songs bring them to tears every time, but their hope is that by hearing the songs in the privacy of their home or car, time and time again, when they hear that song in public, they don't have a complete meltdown. This might be helpful for you. I'm just offering possible suggestions to aid you in finding the light you're searching for.

**Reflect.** Think about the qualities and characteristics of your sibling that you most admire, and find ways to adapt them into your life. Incorporate the best qualities of your sibling into how you carry out your life. I try to live daily with this mantra: *be* the things you loved most about your loved one.

**Read.** If you enjoy reading, head to the library, get your Kindle loaded up, borrow from friends. Again, find your genre of books, and spend some time reading. Find other grief books; take the parts that resonate with you, and use them to assist you in your grief healing process. Find lighthearted books to take your mind to another place. Grab a mystery, and get engrossed in solving it before the last chapter. Perhaps it's a short read because you know you can't focus for a longer period of time. Maybe it's a book that you don't have to put much thought into; it's just something to take your mind off your grieving for a period of time. If reading is something you've enjoyed in the past, perhaps now is the time to pick that back up.

**Grace.** Offer yourself grace. I cannot stress this enough. It is so easy to doubt and second-guess yourself. It seems second nature to beat yourself up for not acting like you're supposed to. Be gentle with yourself. Be kind to yourself. Offer yourself grace on the good days as well as the bad days. Offering yourself grace is oftentimes easier said than done. Early in my grief journey, I didn't even realize that was an option because I didn't see the outside, bigger picture that was beyond my cocoon. Once I began to notice the world around me, I was aware that some people were expecting me to act in certain ways by "getting over it." Fortunately, I'm living from a place where grace wins, and I want to offer that mindset to you.

# CARING FOR THE GRIEVING

**ERR ON THE SIDE OF CAUTIOUSNESS** when being there for grievers and trying to support them.

If you're like me, I'm sure you've heard plenty of advice for what to do, how to act, and how to handle your grief. One thing I've learned along the way during my grief journey is to be *very* selective and intentional with what I say and do in trying to help or console others who are grieving.

First and foremost, support them. You can do this in many different ways.

- Offer to sit with them. No words are necessary. Sometimes it's just about being there. Just be present.
- Encourage them to talk about their loved one. Let them reminisce, tell stories, and share their memories.
- Share a memory about the person who's gone. Write down your memories so they have it as a keepsake.
- Listen. Just listen. Many times, the person grieving isn't looking for advice; they're just wanting to be heard.
- Have empathy. Remember that *their* feelings are *just that*; you don't need to interject your feelings. Let them feel what they feel.

- Allow them a safe haven to cry. Don't be afraid to cry with them.
- Invite them to do things with you.
- Stay clear of the blanket statement of: "Let me know what I can do." The griever most likely doesn't even know what they need or how you can help. Offer to pick up groceries. Or, better yet, shop for some basic grocery items and drop them off at their house.
- Leave them care packages.
- Offer other practical help, e.g., mow the lawn, shovel the snow, or offer to pick up their kids from school or sports practice. Again, instead of offering, be specific about how you'll help out. Tell them, "I'll be at your house Tuesday to mow your lawn" or "I've got carpool covered for your kids this coming week."
- Use the deceased person's name in conversations.
- Prepare some meals that can be frozen to eat later.
- Offer to take them to upcoming appointments.
- Remember, it's not about you.
- Meet them where they are, not where you think they should be. We don't get to tell someone how to grieve or for how long.
- Continue to check in on them in the weeks, months, and yes, years to come, especially then. All too often people forget once the funeral is done.
- Remember important dates (e.g., birthdays of the deceased, anniversary, angelversary).

Steer away from the typical clichés (here are a few).

- "I know how you feel." (It's not about *you*!)
- "You shouldn't feel _____."
- "Stop crying."
- "At least they're in a better place."

- "You should probably move on; it's been a while now."
- "There's a reason for everything."
- "Keep yourself busy so you don't think about it."
- "Time will heal." (Healing is an individual process.)
- "You're young; you can have other children."
- "You're young, you can remarry."
- "Be glad for the time you did have together."
- "You are strong. Be strong. You have to be strong for _____."
- "Look on the bright side."
- "Keep a stiff upper lip."
- "It's for the best."
- "God doesn't give you more than you can handle."
- "God must have wanted them because they were such a great person."
- "You should _____."
- "You'll get over this."
- "You'll be fine."
- "Be grateful for what you have. (Which one of your relatives are you willing to give up right now?)"

Here are some things to say instead.

- Nothing. You don't have to say anything. Just give them a hug. (You don't have to fill idle time with words.)
- "I wish I had the right words, but I don't. Please know that I care and that I'm here for you."
- "Do you want to talk?"
- "You and your loved ones are in my prayers." (Be careful with this. I'm fine with this but not all are; religion can sometimes be a touchy subject.) Perhaps you could say, "You're in my thoughts" or "You're in my heart."

- "I didn't personally know _____, but based on who you are, he/she must have been pretty special."
- "I'm so sorry." "I can't imagine. Would you like to talk about it?"
- "I can see you're hurting."
- "This must be really hard."
- "How are you feeling?" (There is a fine line with this; many times, grievers don't know how they are feeling.)
- "Can I pray for you?" (Again, know your griever; you certainly don't want to offend them.)
- "Would you like to go for a walk with me?" Or, maybe better, "Let's go for a walk."
- "I'm so sorry this has happened to you."
- "I don't know what to say. How can I help?" (Perhaps this is when you simply specify what you'll do: mow lawn, carpool kids, etc.)
- "Give yourself the time you need to process and heal."
- "I'm here for you."
- "I'm inspired by the way _____ lived his/her life."

# WHERE I AM NOW

**HAVING THE** *ability* to say, "Hindsight is 20/20" is definitely reflective of where I am now on my grief journey. This phrase wasn't even on my vision board, let alone my radar, during the first couple of years. In fact, at the time, I didn't think I'd ever be in a different place emotionally. My grief was so all-encompassing that I was incapable of fast-forwarding to another time. I was unable to catch a glimpse of a future that didn't include despair, darkness, and desolation. I am no longer the same person I was, and that's a good thing, for the most part. The old Kim still resides inside this body; however, she's metamorphosed into a different Kim. This change in personality is something that is hard to describe to someone who has never grieved. Both the old Kim and the different Kim dwell together and would give anything to go back in time to where Duane was still here. I can play the "just one more _____" game, but the reality is that will never be, and so with that in mind, I can allow myself to wish for those things with my heart, but my head has to continue on this healing journey. In the freshness of year one, I was existing at the most basic level. I was in a fog, floundering around, with a plethora of emotions that engulfed every cell in my body, overtaking the essence of me. I didn't see a way out of that gigantic, yet minuscule, dark pit, nor did I want to. The pit seemed to be huge, but at the same time, it felt so tiny and isolating that I was suffocating in that dark pit. At times it felt like a crater had sucked me down inside it, yet at the same time, it felt as though it was this tiny prison cell that was desolate, lonely, and claustrophobic.

Although many people tried to throw me ropes, send me a lifeboat, or drop down an oxygen mask, I didn't have the desire or energy to respond in what could have been a life-altering way. If you're at this point in the book, I don't need to reiterate my year one, as you've likely already lived something similar to it. Year one sucked; yes, that's blunt, but I don't really have a delicate way to describe it. Perhaps this is where you currently reside. I understand. No judgment here, whatsoever.

Believe me, the second year wasn't always a walk in the park either, but it included more and larger glimpses of hope. There were definitely times where I felt as if I was taking giant steps forward, just to hear someone say, "You didn't say, 'Mother'; may I?" and I was forced to take ten steps back. Some days I was proud as a peacock because I felt that I was conquering the days in stride. And then, out of nowhere, an enormous movie screen was projecting in slow motion the rawness of Duane's passing, and all the anguish resurfaced, toying with my heart and head. It was as if I were being taunted to play Chutes and Ladders. Would I climb back up the ladder using the tools that had helped me get to this point? Or would I slide right back down the chute into the pit?

> "Somedays I feel as if I'm conquering the world in your honor; and some days I feel as if I'm lost in the heartache of your absence" (author unknown).

> "Not a day goes by that I don't look at your picture and smile. Or cry. Or both" (unknown).

There is nothing easy about a grief journey. What I realized, however, was that during this time period, I liked the feeling of happiness and joy, even a sense of peacefulness, and I wanted to experience more of that. It was during year two that I revisited my gratitude practice. With intention, I did my best to search for reasons to be grateful each and every day. Some days, I had to get out my magnifying glass because listing a gratitude was like finding a needle in a haystack. However, most days, I was able to successfully bookend my days with gratitude.

> "When you choose to live your life from a place of gratitude, you also choose to live a life of joy and abundance" (yourjoyologist.com).

For me, practicing gratitude provides an experience of truly *feeling* good in my life. The more I practiced it, the more I was at peace.

> "Thankfulness creates gratitude which generates contentment that causes peace" (Todd Stocker).

It was also during year two that I rekindled my love for writing. As a middle schooler, I enjoyed writing and periodically continued to dabble in it from time to time, writing a poem, or creating party invitations. It was in 2021 to 2022 that I began writing a chapter for *The Badass Within* book collaboration. Writing my chapter, "The Roller Coaster Ride of Grief," allowed me to bring a voice to all the raw emotions that had literally consumed me mind, body, and soul. The writing process was therapeutic for me and definitely helped my healing process.

As year two played out, I began to evolve, having (or should I say needing) a mission and a purpose. I did not want my pain to go in vain. I knew how desperately I had needed and wanted to be heard, validated, and seen as a sibling griever (or any griever for that matter), and I wanted to be someone who could provide empathy and compassion from an "I've been in similar shoes" perspective. (I do not feel I have the right to tell anyone, "I know what you're going through," as I will never know exactly what it feels like to be them.) All grief is valid. *Always*. I wanted to find ways to let siblings, as well as other grievers, know that what they are feeling is OK. And it is definitely OK to not be OK.

I desperately wanted to provide others with a safe haven to talk, share, cry, smile, and feel validated as a griever. So I started a grief support group and acted as the group's facilitator. Neither our town nor the surrounding area had anything like this when I needed it; I was determined to make it happen. I made it my mission to be able to provide this opportunity not only for our community but for others in surrounding communities. Together, we've all leaned on each other and are still finding ways to grow and heal on our grief journeys. I'm happy to say we've welcomed many new faces over the last couple of years. By nature, I like to serve others, and this is one way I can fill my cup. Somewhere during year two, I began thirsting for something to rehydrate my weary soul; I wanted to enjoy life again. I wanted to smile, have fun, and "be" again. There was a lot of inner work that took place between ground zero (Duane's passing) and year two. I dug deeper into my faith, into my hopes and dreams for my future, and ultimately, I had to intentionally make some decisions. What do I want for the rest of *my* life? Would I get back in the ring of life again (as battered and scarred as I was), or would I succumb to catastrophic desolation? I had too much life ahead of me to do anything but fight my way back. I desperately wanted to witness the world around me in vivid colors again, as opposed to the gray and black canvas that had been my backdrop as well as focal point for so long. The more peace and contentment I felt, the more I craved it, and I *needed* more of it. I wanted another "hit" of those feel-good endorphins; I wanted more happiness hormones! (What a shocker that was; who knew I'd be craving something wonderful ever again!)

Once I allowed myself to understand that experiencing joy and happiness again in my life didn't negate or diminish the relationship I had with Duane, it was like an epiphany of sorts. It was OK to be happy. It was OK to laugh. But it was also OK to cry. It was OK to be sad. My heart certainly isn't less sad, but it's sad less often. Nowadays, the sadness doesn't typically carry the same intensity as it used to, but it still carries the same volume. I've heard it said that the level of grief is equivalent to the level of love that once was. My love for Duane hasn't lessened by any means; in fact, it has deepened.

"The loss is immeasurable but so is the love left behind" (unknown).

I appreciate, even more, what we had as the essence of us. Now, as I recall memories of our lifetime together, I allow myself to *teleport* back into that time and place. It's as if I'm inhaling the memories with hypersensitive awareness, and for the most part, that brings me significant joy instead of an intense sadness.

> "There is another side of grief where the tears still flow but not as often, where memories bring smiles, not just sadness. Where blessings are recognized, not just struggles, where joy is present, not just sorrow, where you are remembered, not just mourned" (author unknown).

Wow, just to hear myself say that—I am definitely not where I used to be on this grief journey.

Year two brought smiles, laughter, joy, peace, hope, and contentment, along with tears, anxiousness, loneliness, and an emptiness. However, the good outweighed the bad, and I *liked* that! This feeling was the catalyst for me wanting more of that! Which leads me to where I am now. So much has contributed to me being where I am now. First and foremost, I have to give God the credit where credit is due in my life. My faith journey has definitely contributed to where I am now. Time and time again, God proved to me that I was never alone, that He was actually carrying me through the eye of the storm. For me, there is no other way to explain how I got from point A to where I am now at point Q. As I said, it's a journey, and I'm still traveling along the path, so if point Z is a destination, I won't arrive. Grief is a continuous journey.

> "I'll forever credit God, He pulled me out of some really dark places" (author unknown).

The unconditional love and never-ending support from my whole BarkStrong family and friends (aka, BarkStrong network) has been phenomenal. My ability to be in contact with my bereavement counselor when the need arises has been a tremendous help, knowing that I have her to fall back on in times of need. My writing has been therapeutic and kept me on the path of healing in my grief journey. Shortly after the launch of *The Badass Within*, I jumped on board as co-lead author and wrote another chapter, this time, for *Graceful Growth*. It was in *Graceful Growth* that I brought a voice to the difficulty of losing my dad twice (once to Alzheimer's/dementia and the second to his actual passing).

This is my Facebook post the day of Dad's private funeral and burial, December 6, 2020.

> Today is the day I'm supposed to say goodbye; I can't do that, Dad. I will, however, tell you how much I love you, tell you how proud I am of the man you are, tell you how proud I am to be Doug Bark's daughter, tell you how much I appreciate who you are and what you've done for me and countless others, tell you that you inspire me every day to be the best I can be, tell you that I will remain BarkStrong and carry on the legacy you and Duane have left the blueprint for, tell you I will take care of Mom, tell you that I will make sure our Bark

family stays intact and continues to cherish, support, and love each other with every ounce of our being, tell you that I will be true to my faith and trust in God's ways and God's plans, tell you that through all the tears, my heart and mind are full of a lifetime of memories that will re-anchor my soul, tell you that I know without a shadow of a doubt you and my Big Bro are watching over me, protecting me, and guiding me with your love, tell you that I will see you again and I know you'll bear hug me tight with that wink in your eye. Please have a bowl of ice cream ready and a spoonful of brown sugar! I love you! ~Daddy's Little Girl.

Helping others along their grief journey has also contributed to my ability to be where I am now. For me, serving others in meaningful ways brings me joy, and who doesn't want more joy! My gratitude practice has expanded; not only do I recognize gratitudes at the beginning and end of my day, but I find many things to be grateful for throughout my days. Gratitude is a breeding ground for more gratitude.

Where I am now has purpose, or should I say, *I have purpose* in where I am now. I purposefully spend time with family and friends, truly inhaling and absorbing the moments. With intention, I slow down, taking time to enjoy instead of going through the motions and being oblivious to the beauty and goodness around me. I can honestly say that where I am now is a complete 180 from where I used to be. The old Kim's foundational pieces are still here, but grief has changed me in many ways.

> "The reality is you will grieve forever. You will not 'get over' the loss of a loved one; you will learn to live with it. You will heal and you will rebuild yourself around the loss you have suffered. You will be whole again but you will never be the same again. Nor should you be the same nor should you want to" (Elizabeth Kübler-Ross).

My guess is that you're finding the same to be true for you. Is grief still a part of my life? Yes. Will grief always be a part of my life? Yes. Just like waves washing up on the sand, grief changes the placement of the sand, but the beach still remains.

The following is an excerpt from *The Badass Within*.

I still have moments and days of sadness, tears, and a heavy heart. However, I'm back! I have hope in my life again. I have a loving God who will always be by my side, no matter what storms of life are ahead of me.

I didn't write this section to make you feel bad or make you feel lesser than; remember, with grief there is no measuring stick. Your journey belongs to you, and mine belongs to me, and the chances are that we are not in the exact moment in time of grieving. Instead, I've written this to bring you hope, be your beacon of light, and let you know that as time goes by, not only does grief change in *how* it shows up for you, but it also changes *you,* in how you present yourself to the world. What *I've* found is that grief no longer controls me; instead, I'm now able to manage it better. Contrary to what some people think and say, time does not take the grief away; grief will always be a part of your life because this was someone you loved tremendously, shared a history with, and had a bond with that nobody else had.

> "However long it takes, your heart and your mind will carve out a new life amid this weirdly devastated landscape. Little by little, pain and love will find ways to coexist" (Megan Devine).

I've recognized that, with time, the grief no longer loiters in every single corner of my whereabouts, like an escaped convict waiting to take me prisoner. It no longer gashes me open with jagged shards of glass, knifing me open, revealing my insides, and leaving me hemorrhaging and blood-soaked. Grief no longer knocks me over like a tsunami leaving me disoriented and breathless; the impact of grief is more gentle and mellow now. Grief no longer lurks around every corner; instead, it randomly meets me on the street. I can choose to sit and chat with it, invite it over for an eight-course meal, or I can say I don't have time right now, but we'll touch base soon. I no longer have tsunami tidal waves of grief. I've learned to surf and ride the waves as they ebb and flow in and out of my life. Heck, I can even take tranquil walks in the soft sand as the water rescinds back into the ocean now. If someone had told me three years ago that my life would, and could, look like this, I would have told them they were deliriously insane!

I can't pinpoint a specific moment where all of this changed from me being encapsulated inside that cocoon to me now being unconfined and able to move through life with less restrictions. There are times when I don't feel like spreading my wings and showing up beautiful for the world. Some moments I'd rather fold up my wings and camouflage myself, blending into my personal surroundings. But guess what—*that's OK!*

If I can leave you with anything, I want to leave you with warmth, a sense of peace, and true hope for what's yet to come in your life. Honor your loved one. Embrace what the two of you had. Remember that grief is a journey, not some arbitrary destination that is reached and checked off. Most of all, know that you are not alone.

> "The final stage of healing is using what happens to you to help other people" (Gloria Steinem).

Feel free to connect with me via my website: mindful-empowerment.net.

# KIM'S PERSONAL RESOURCES

**THIS IS A SECTION** of other quotes, poems, and Facebook posts that helped me during my grief journey. These quotes and poems spoke directly to my heart—I was the sister who was grieving the loss of her Big Bro, and nobody else seemed to understand. I want to offer these helpful tidbits to you in hopes that they might touch a place in your heart as well.

"I'll always be your sister. You'll always be my hero" (author unknown).

"There are losses that rearrange the world. Deaths that change the way you see everything, grief that tears everything down. Pain that transports you to an entirely different universe, even while everyone else thinks nothing has really changed" (Megan Devine).

"Let God turn your pain into purpose, your grief into growth" (Diana C. Derringer).

"Sometimes it's very hard to release what's making you sad because it's the same thing that brought you much joy" (unknown).

"If you have nothing in life but a loving brother, you're rich" (unknown author).

"It's OK to feel like your loss is the worst loss in the world. It is the worst loss in *your* world" (author unknown).

"The loss of a brother or sister is not small, unimportant, or invisible. In fact, it's quite the opposite. I call sibling loss "the loss of a lifetime" because who else do we expect to have relationships with that stretch our entire lives?" (author unknown).

"Once you've accepted the loss of a sibling, there is nothing life can throw your way that is too difficult to let go of ... nothing. You suffered the loss of someone so precious that it left you paralyzed and even difficult to breathe ... with sadness so immense that it brought you actual, physical pain, and there were times when you believed YOU TOO may die from the intensity of it all. But you are still here. You survived the unimaginable. You can accept ... ANYTHING" (Carrie Beaugrand).

## KIM'S PERSONAL RESOURCES

*I Am My Brothers Sister*

I am my brother's sister
To some that may not mean much
But we were always there for each other
Especially when times were tough
Now that he is gone
I am left to carry on
Trying to be strong…
No, I am strong
Because I am my brother's sister
He taught me so much
And that, no one can touch
Because I am my brother's sister
I learned to stand tall
Throughout it all
No matter what life throws at me
I'll make it through, you'll see

(Author unknown.)

# KIM'S PERSONAL WRITING

**THIS IS ONE WAY** I could, in a paragraph or two, release some of the grief. These are a sample of Facebook posts that I wrote during this time. They were a way for me to speak from my heart and became my own personal therapy sessions. My hope is that within these personal writings you can find a safety net for whenever you are ready for it. And that it ultimately can bring you hope, peace, and comfort during your journey.

## October 14, 2020

> "I've got your back, Sis" ... Thanks, Big Bro ~ you knew we would need people to lean on. You spent your life influencing people and making a difference for others. And now your network of people, whose lives you've touched, has become our safety net and our place to find comfort. Just another example of you always being there and taking care of those you love. Love you, Big Bro.

## December 7, 2020

"2 minutes, 2 days, 2 weeks, 2 months, 2 years ... it doesn't matter what increment of time, I will always wish we had more time, more laughter, more heart-to-heart talks, more fun, more memories, more hugs, more I Love You's.

What a reunion it must have been when Dad joined you.

I love you, and I am rich because you're my Big Bro.

## October 7, 2021

A year ago today I was left with the question of how to navigate this life without my Big Bro. There is no manual for any of us when dealing with the death of a loved one.

"Time heals," "carry on," and other such intentions didn't (and still don't) resonate with me. What does resonate is offering myself grace to feel what I feel and honor those feelings, recognize them for what they are, and let them ebb and flow like the tide.

Although today is raw, and it feels like someone ripped off the Band-Aid, I know I'll get through it BarkStrong. The hurt hurts immensely when the love runs so deep.

During this last year, I've been embraced with genuine love, care, and concern from family, friends, coworkers, acquaintances, even people I didn't even know. (This is just another way that my Big Bro continues to love and protect me.)

Big Bro, I love you and I miss you.

As a family, we are stronger together. We will draw strength from our faith and continue to welcome the ability to lean in and lean on our family and friends.

Until we meet again, Big Bro 🖤🖤~

Love ya,
Sis

# WITH GRATITUDE

**DUANE—THANK YOU, BIG BRO,** for always having my back. You are everything I could have asked for in a big brother and then some! Your love for me encompassed so many things—protection, guidance, encouragement, unconditional love, and so much more. My life is richer because of our bond.

Dad and Mom—You taught me *how* to love and how to *be* loved. Thank you for showing me what unconditional love is and what it means to be BarkStrong. You've always believed in me, supported me, and wanted the best for me, and I thank you for that. Throughout my life, you've watched with pride and cheered me on as I have chased my dreams.

My family—First and foremost, I love you. Thank you for your never-wavering, never-faltering, unconditional love. It is inside this protective encasement of sincere devotion that I find my peace, comfort, and contentment. Your love and support have allowed me the reassurance of chasing my dreams and knowing I will always have a safety net, should I need one, in whatever endeavors I choose to pursue. You've been my biggest fans during times of celebrations, and more importantly, my biggest source of strength when I needed you most. As we have added members to our family through the years, my heart has expanded in exponential ways. I thank God for each of you; you're my world and my heartbeat. I am truly blessed to call you mine.

Duane's family (Pam, Brad, Brian, Brittany and their families)—my Big Bro has definitely provided me with the best of the best. I want to thank each of you for having my back, no matter what. I know without a shadow of a doubt that we will continue to walk through this life, in BarkStrong ways, leaning on each other. I love each of you and your presence in my life is a blessing. And for that, I am forever grateful.

My BarkStrong network of family and friends (too many to name individually)—A huge thank you to each and every one of you. You've not only propped me up when my foundation crumbled, witnessing my lowest of lows, but you've also been right beside me, cheering me on with your encouragement, sharing my joys, and celebrating my accomplishments. It's with you that I have found what true friendship looks and feels like. Thank you.

Kim Rosenbrook—Thank you to my namesake for the beautiful, front cover photo of Duane and me. As a photographer, you were able to perfectly capture the essence of us, and for that, I am forever grateful. God blessed us with each other and it is my honor to be your KAB1. I love you, KAB2!

My publishing team—Thanks to everyone on my publishing team, especially to you, Amy Collette. You believed in me and encouraged me to write from my heart, guiding me with the utmost of compassion along the way. Amy, thank you for pouring your heart and soul not only into this book, but to me as a friend as well. I could not have done this without you. Another special thanks goes to Victoria Wolf. You took my vision and brought it to life on the front cover—a uniqueness that is solely mine.

# ABOUT THE AUTHOR

**KIM BARK WHITE** is a retired teacher and mindfulness coach who founded Mindful Empowerment, a company dedicated to helping others through different mentorships, such as academic tutor, reiki master, speaker, life mentor, and a grief support facilitator. As a mindfulness coach, Kim was trained and certified through the Growing Minds™ curriculum.

She is a two-time best-selling author, contributing to *The Badass Within* and *Graceful Growth*, sharing her personal story of grief through the loss of both her brother and father. She takes pride in meeting people where they are, empowering them to unleash the best versions of themselves. In honor of her dad and big brother's examples, Kim passionately devotes herself to making a difference and leaving an impact. Her passions and purpose have come together with her God-given talents as she continues to serve others with compassion, understanding, and genuine concern.

Kim holds her BS in education from the University of Wisconsin, Platteville. Kim lives with her husband, Al, in Wisconsin, spending much of their free time with their three children and their families.

# CONNECT WITH KIM

mindful-empowerment.net

Facebook: mindfulempowermentkw and KimWhite

# The Badass Within

By Erin Baer and Kim Bark White, co-author

**YOU MIGHT SUSPECT** that there is a Badass within you, but she's been hiding for a long time. She might feel beaten down by life. She might feel beaten down by grief or abuse or health issues or trauma. But you know she's still there somehow, and you're wondering how to let her out.

The writers in *The Badass Within* were wondering the same thing, until they came to a point in their lives where they had to confront the "elephant in the room"—that thing that was holding them back and holding them down. Fifteen women share stories that are personal, real, and courageous. You will witness their sadness, joy, and strength. It's in their sharing that they release the chains of the past and unleash the badass within. Their hope is that you, too, will be inspired to discover the Badass within and let her shine.

## PRAISES

"*The Badass Within* is an amazing collaboration of experiences compiled by strong, badass women. From grief, infertility, unhealthy relationships and more, you won't finish the book without relating to the authors, feeling less alone, and finding a glimmer of light in your own daily battles." —Brie Kirsch

"The amazing author of *From Beaten to Badass* has done it again! Erin Baer brings us *The Badass Within*. The amazing women in this book share stories that are tough, hopeful and relatable. Every person who is struggling to find their badass within needs this book.

This is a book that I will keep on the shelf for the times when I need to gather courage and strength. Get ready to be inspired..." —Colette Smith

"What an amazing way to inspire others to never stop believing in themselves, to always keep going, and never ever feel like they're alone. Every story sheds light on the fact that each day is a new day, and to never ever take it for granted." —Missy Cornwell-Nichols

"*The Badass Within* is a beautiful collaboration among women who are courageous enough to be vulnerable and open with their audience, with a united goal of helping others. While each of their stories is unique, the common theme of strength, perseverance, and never giving up is present throughout and everyone can find a story to relate to." —Vanessa Rush, Ph.D.

"These are some brave individuals that have bared their struggles, pain and sorrow. They have found ways to work through that and have become better people. You are not alone! Find YOUR badass within!" —Kim S.

"From the first story to the last story, *The Badass Within* is a powerful read. I was crying, shouting, praying and cheering these ladies on as I was drawn into their amazing, powerful and challenging lives. They all have faced adversities that would have crippled most people but they dug deep within themselves and moved forward. From addiction, mental, physical abuse and illness, unhealthy marriages and even death, they knew they had something in them that said, "Don't Give Up" and they didn't, even when others tried to hold them back. I pray I don't have to face any situation remotely similar but if I do, I will turn to them for their message of hope." —Beth Bilton

"Heart breaking to heartwarming. Struggling to strength. Raw to restrained to resilient. Suffering to survivor.

Beautifully written and eloquently articulated stories that struck chords within my soul. These women's stories ignited my inner fire of badasseary. For so long, I have felt so alone in my own journey. I used to hear other women's stories and feel that my own story wasn't "as bad" as others. While I am proud of the mountains I have climbed over, I never felt worthy of the same praise as others. Until this book. About halfway through, the proverbial lightbulb flickered on. It doesn't matter the experiences we have been through. It matters what we do with it, how we handle it, how we grow, how we embrace our inner badass. And how we hold our heads high and walk into the storm with fire in our eyes and scream, "I am worthy! Watch me be the Badass I am."" —Danielle Danforth

"Phenomenal stories from women who are true badasses! I read it entirely in one sitting, and shed more than a few tears along the way. Real, raw, and honest." — Carrie Linder

"A powerful read for women of all ages. The authors aren't superstars, they're real women who have faced real problems but have come through it and found their inner badass. Our society places so much shame on abuse, addiction, and mental health struggles. The Badass Within authors openly discuss their experiences, which will undoubtedly help so many other women who share the same struggles." – Amy B. Jones, School Psychologist

# *Graceful Growth*

By Erin Baer and Kim Bark White

**THIS BOOK IS FILLED** with life stories and life experiences people don't want to talk about; "the elephant in the room." But avoiding the truth is the very reason our mental and emotional well-being has been traumatized. Graceful Growth is filled with passionate and compassionate life-transforming experiences that come from way down deep in the heart of each author.

## PRAISES

"This book is a must read for those who truly want to be freed, for when we face our truths, we free our minds, our bodies, and our souls. What we go through doesn't define us, what we experience can make us stronger. This book has transformed my heart. We all need love, affection, and a sense of unconditional, communal support to know we are not alone on this journey through life. We need one another. Every story in this book is a head-on confrontation with the elephant in the room that encourages us to embrace our truth, to take a stand and speak up for ourselves, unleash the badass within, and with balance, be graceful in our growth." —Marissa L. Bloedoorn, M.Sc., DTM Master DISC Behavioral Analyst and Best-Selling Publisher and Author

"Grief. A short word. One syllable. Basic. Simple. Except there's nothing basic or simple about the grieving process. Step inside *Graceful Growth* and follow these amazing women as they journey through their various experiences of grief and come out on the other side empowered, stronger and unrelentingly full of grace." —Sally Root

"What a powerful read! I found myself having to stop and compose myself a few times. These ladies' stories really made me take a step back and reevaluate how I've handled loss and setbacks in my own life. They all chose to keep moving forward and use their hardships to grow and learn and become stronger. They chose to see hope and light where many would only see darkness and sorrow. I personally am going to keep this book close and look to it for encouragement when I start doubting my ability to keep going when I want to curl up and quit.

Thank you all for putting these experiences into words. I hope they help people who are struggling. They certainly helped me gain a new perspective." —Nicole Kocian

"I sit here with tears streaming down my face as I read the last page of *Graceful Growth*. Each chapter takes you on a journey as the authors share their powerful stories. I am in awe of the strength and courage they found within themselves to grow beyond the pain of grief and loss. Thank you to the authors for sharing your stories, your book will bring hope and inspiration to all who read it!" —Cindy Doss

"This phenomenal collection of stories is a testament that proves when you have faith and perseverance, you can overcome any of life's unimaginable obstacles. I felt each author's pain and heartbreak through their well-written, heart-wrenching words. I highly recommend you read this book with a box of tissues nearby." —Carrie Linder

"I was so deeply touched by the stories these women shared. They all experienced incredible losses and wrote about them to help inspire others to grow through their grief. Mission accomplished! I guarantee there is at least one story in this book that any reader could relate to. These women have bared their souls, sharing how they worked through their grief and came out on the other side. I was incredibly moved by each of their stories and so impressed with how open they were about the tragedies they lived (and grew) through. This book shows that the process of grieving is not a straight line from A to B and not the same for every person; but you can weather the storm and come out stronger than you were before. We have all experienced some sort of loss so this book is a must read." —Amy Jones

www.ingramcontent.com/pod-product-compliance
Lightning Source LLC
Chambersburg PA
CBHW031404160426
43196CB00007B/887